An old song says: "Heaven's sounding sweeter all the time." You will definitely feel this way after reading *The Draw of Heaven*. Pastor Sharon opens her life, her heart and God's Word in a way that will inspire you eternally. From the intimate account of the death of her husband, to the power of God's forever promises, you will be blessed by this book.

—*Dr. Billy Wilson*
President, Oral Roberts University

Sharon Daugherty is without a doubt one of the most outstanding friends I have ever known. She has impacted my life with her worship, with her wisdom, with her love. I consider her a hero in the Body of Christ.

I'm delighted that she shared about the death of Billy Joe in *The Draw of Heaven*. Those of us who knew Billy Joe admired him so much as we admire Sharon in this time. Truly, when she says the Holy Spirit is a shock absorber, He really is. Her faith has revealed and shows it.

The Draw of Heaven is important for all of us because we need to know about Heaven. We talk about Heaven but do we really know about it and do we understand that God has such a draw on our lives and that this life is temporary and Heaven is eternal? God bless you, Sharon, for sharing your passion, your experiences and the promise of God's words to all of us.

—*Dr. Marilyn Hickey*
President and Founder, Marilyn Hickey Ministries

Heaven is defined as "the abode of blissful life after death" by *Webster's Dictionary*. Sharon Daugherty has written the probing and penetrating book, *The Draw of Heaven*, that opens the gates of heaven and gives a guided tour of that eternal city where there are no tears, no pain, no suffering, no death for the former things have passed away. You will enjoy *The Draw of Heaven*!

—*Pastor John Hagee*
Cornerstone Church

Thank you, Pastor Sharon, for sharing your story of victory in the face of an overwhelming time. This book will help us all realize the goodness of God on earth and our glorious future in Him. What a glorious tour of Heaven you've given us!

—*Pastor George Pearsons*
Eagle Mountain International Church

Heaven is a real place. The people there are enjoying life without the sorrow attached to this world. For those of us who are left on earth to deal with the loss of someone who has gone to such a wonderful place, it can be a challenge. Sharon Daugherty will teach you, in this book, what you need to know. She is a woman whom I've known for years. She is a mature woman of God who will help you greatly.

—*Bishop Keith A. Butler*
Senior Pastor, Word of Faith International
Christian Center, Southfield, Michigan
Founder & President of Keith Butler Ministries

Sharon Daugherty's book will spur on anyone in pursuit of Heaven. Sharing from some of her deepest experiences of walking with God through the death of her husband, Billy Joe Daugherty, Sharon offers treasures of wisdom that will help every reader choose God's higher ways when walking through life's most challenging experiences.

As you read, I believe you will be greatly impacted by the truths the Lord revealed to Sharon through her husband's early passing and by the profound revelation of life over death she experienced as she put her trust wholly in Him. I am a personal fan of Sharon Daugherty, and this book confirms everything I hold to be true about her and her unwavering faith. This is the book for anyone who is crying out to know eternal truths about those in Christ who have passed into eternity. I cannot recommend it highly enough.

—Rick Renner
Senior Pastor, Moscow Good News Church
in the Former Soviet Union
and Founder/Director of Good News
Association of Pastors and Churches

Sharon Daugherty is one of the most amazing women I know. A tremendous wife to the husband she adored for years, a pastor's wife who is respected by all and a mother of grown children. Sharon cared for Billy Joe and fought alongside him until he went to heaven. Then she carried on the job of pastoring the church. I have been amazed at her strength and am so proud of her. Her book will bless you tremendously. I salute her.

— Dodie Osteen
Co-Founder of Lakewood Church

Billy Joe Daugherty represented integrity, purity, and passion for souls in his life. Sharon Daugherty represents honor, faith, and stability as she carries on the faith message from a supernatural standpoint. Regardless of your circumstances and what you might be dealing with in life, this book will bring you into a new level of understanding, peace, joy, purpose...and Victory! It will increase your belief in the supernatural and strengthen your faith as you walk out all that God has planned for you in spite of life's greatest challenges. Heaven is not just in our future; it touches us now!

—Larry Stockstill
Pastor, Bethany Church, Baton Rouge, Louisiana

the DRAW of HEAVEN

the DRAW *of* HEAVEN

SUPERNATURAL INSIGHTS TO LIFE'S HARDEST QUESTIONS

SHARON DAUGHERTY

HONOR NET
PUBLISHERS
SAPULPA, OK

Published by HonorNet Publishers

P. O. Box 910
Sapulpa, OK 74067
Website: honornet.net

CONTENTS

PART 3:

HEAVEN—OUR FINAL HOME

FOREWORD

THE SPIRITUAL REALM OFTEN goes unnoticed, and yet it is as tangible as the words on this page. A glimpse of the unseen can shift our focus from earthbound distractions to eternal purposes.

> *As for us, we have all of these great witnesses who encircle us like clouds, each affirming faith's reality. So we must let go of every wound that has pierced us and the sin we so easily fall into. Then we will be able to run life's marathon race with passion and determination, for the path has been already marked out before us. We look away from the natural realm and we fasten our gaze onto Jesus who birthed faith within us and who leads us forward into faith's perfection. His example is this: Because his heart was filled with the joy of knowing that you would be his, he endured the agony of the cross and conquered its humiliation, and now sits exalted at the right hand of the throne of God!*
>
> —HEBREWS 12:1–2, TPT

Those who have gone on to heaven began something we are to finish. They are praying for us and cheering us on to our victory. But there is a battle in the heavenlies, and its goal is to paralyze us from moving forward and reaping a harvest.

When our dear friend Pastor Billy Joe joined the cloud of witnesses, it would have been easy for Pastor Sharon, his beloved wife, to sink into her grief. She chose instead to fix her gaze upon the Lord and to push forward in her heavenly commission.

When we encounter trials, we have one vital weapon on which to rely: God's Word, which is our living, invincible sword. With Scripture as her rock, Pastor Sharon realized that the Holy Spirit longed to give her counsel, strength, stability, and an assurance that could not be taken away. This revelation has positioned her to help countless others find their sure foundation in the presence of God.

If you have been struggling with the absence of a loved one, allow this book to strengthen you. We are so thankful that Sharon courageously poured her journey of healing onto these pages. *The Draw of Heaven* will fill you with truth and hope. Our prayer is that you will push through life's battles with endurance and live for Jesus and the gospel—just like Pastors Billy Joe and Sharon.

We have been deeply impacted and amazed by Pastor Billy Joe and Sharon's great legacy. Billy Joe's life was a seed that produced a magnificent harvest. We are so proud of Pastor Sharon's faithfulness in expanding what God deposited and began in Pastor Billy Joe. Her story vividly reveals that faithfulness is not in maintaining, but in multiplying what has been entrusted to us.

—John & Lisa Bevere
Founders of Messenger International
Colorado Springs, Colorado

INTRODUCTION

Is there something beyond our own mind's reasoning that draws upon our hearts, particularly when a Christian comes close to death's door?

Have you ever wondered why some strong, committed, faith-filled Christians pass into eternity sooner than others expected? I believe there are different circumstances surrounding each individual life. Sometimes the scripture is quoted from Deuteronomy 29:29 (NKJV): "The secret things belong to the LORD our God...." However, the rest of that scripture says, "But those things which are revealed belong to us and to our children...." This lets us know that God can reveal answers to our questions when we draw near to Him with an open heart to hear His thoughts.

When my husband died at age 57, there were many people who questioned why. He had given his life to love and serve God and reach people with the Good News of Jesus Christ. He was also a man of faith. He taught faith and victory in Jesus. He guarded his conversation to speak with faith. He guarded his heart from unforgiveness. He prayed for many people who received healing miracles and many other miracles in their lives. He had an impact upon people—young and old around the world—because he was driven with compassion and a sense of responsibility in fulfilling the Great Commission.

I remember standing by my husband's bed and sensing the presence of angels in his room. Could it be that when a person gets close to death that there is a draw of heaven upon his or her life? I believe this to be true.

This book is to encourage the reader to know that there is a draw of heaven upon our lives. It is also to help anyone who is struggling to find answers to the following questions:

- *Why?*
- *What went wrong?*
- *We were doing all we knew to do.*
- *Maybe if we had just done this other thing.*
- *Maybe if we had not done a particular thing.*

Or, possibly you have thought, "Somehow God failed, or somehow I failed in some way."

Have you ever thought that it might not have been about what you did or didn't do? Have you considered the thought that heaven has a draw upon our lives as believers?

I do not claim to have all the answers to your questions, but I know through my own experience that you can find peace through drawing to the Lord and allowing Him to help you process through the season of life that you are now in.

—Pastor Sharon Daugherty

Part 1

FACING THE DEATH OF A LOVED ONE

Chapter 1

SHOCKED BUT
NOT SHAKEN

IT WAS IN THE early hours of Sunday morning, November 22, 2009, when our family and friends were gathered around my husband's hospital bed as we watched and prayed for him. Gran Gran (Billy Joe's mom); myself; Ruthie and her husband, Adam; John; Sarah and Caleb, Isaac and Lizzie; the newlyweds, Paul and Ashley; Billy Joe's brother Jack; and various friends were there.

We were in a hospital out of state that specialized in treating leukemia and lymphoma diseases.

Two of our children had been overseas in ministry. Our oldest daughter, Sarah, her husband, Caleb, and their two children, Isaac and Lizzie, had been living as missionaries based in Hong Kong for two years and had just arrived the day before. Our youngest son, Paul, and his wife, Ashley, had gone to Russia to speak at a pastors' conference and had been notified to return immediately, so they had just arrived that day.

It seemed as though Billy Joe was waiting for all of his family to be together around his bed before slipping into eternity. He had not been able to communicate for about five days because he was so weak and was medically hooked up to tubes.

When the medical support system began working against his body, they had to unhook the various tubes. He squeezed the hands of our family members as we stood around him praying and talking to him. Then at 4:30 a.m. he passed over into eternity.

Over the weeks leading up to this moment, we had prayed Scripture and believed for him to be raised up to health and wholeness, continuing to live here on earth. We had a CD player that played healing scriptures and songs to minister to him as well.

Billy Joe had not wanted people to talk negatively regarding his physical condition, so he had asked me not to tell people about his illness until three months before he passed. He was fighting the fight of faith all the way. I honored his request, except I asked months earlier if I could share some insight of his condition with our family and share with a few friends closest to us so they could pray. I knew I needed the prayer support.

Many in our congregation could tell something was wrong and would come up and say that they were praying for him, for which I am grateful. Once we shared about the illness publicly, people contacted us from all around the world, letting us know they were praying, fasting, and holding prayer meetings to pray for him. Our congregation had been praying.

I Prayed for Billy Joe to Be Resurrected

On the morning of November 22, 2009, our staff was preparing for our regular Sunday church services. Right before Billy Joe passed,

I thought about Hebrews 11:35, which says, "[By faith] women received their dead raised to life again...." I believed this scripture gave me permission to call Billy Joe back.

After each of our family members had taken time to say good-bye to Billy Joe, I asked to be alone with him. I began to read aloud the resurrection scriptures and stories from the Bible of people who had been raised from the dead. I prayed in the Spirit, and I worshipped God, reminding Him of His Word from Isaiah 43:26 (ASV): "Put me in remembrance; let us plead together: set thou forth thy cause, that thou mayest be justified."

Like a lawyer who pleads the case of his client, we can declare God's Word in prayer as we see ourselves in the courtroom spiritually speaking as we contend against the opposing lawyer, the devil. I believe God, the righteous Judge, hears our statements of His Word as we release our faith in that Word.

I leaned my body over Billy Joe's body as I prayed. Toward the end of three hours as I was worshiping God and singing, "See His Glory Come Down," "We Exalt Thee," and "Jesus, There's Just Something About That Name," I heard a distant choir singing with me in four-part harmony. It was beautiful. Each time I breathed, they breathed. When I stopped, they stopped. I knew it was angels singing.

Then I began singing the chorus of the song, "With All I Am," which says, "Jesus, I believe in You. Jesus, I belong to You. You're the reason that I live, the reason that I sing. Jesus, I believe in You. Jesus, I belong to You. You're the reason that I live, the reason that I sing with all I am."

As soon as I started singing this chorus, the choir stopped singing. I paused and asked the Lord why they stopped. I heard Him say, "Sharon, they can't sing this one with you. You're on your own with this song, because this is a confession of your own faith that you are committed to Me, even when things don't go as you planned."

I looked down at Billy Joe's face, and he had this big smile that had just remained there. I knew he was telling me that he was happy, healed, and at rest with Jesus.

As I've read stories of people who have had out-of-body experiences of going to heaven and coming back, each of them has said that once they left their body it was so wonderful that they didn't want to return. Revelation 14:13 says, "Blessed are the dead which die in the Lord...that they may rest from their labours; and their works do follow them."

I knew then that Billy Joe had gotten a glimpse of the other side before he passed, and that he had felt a release from earth to go to his eternal destiny. I also believe that when a Christian gets close to death and is physically weak, there is a draw of heaven upon his or her life. Those who have labored on earth enter into a rest, and they get the joy of seeing the fruit of their labor and so much more. They see Jesus— the One who saved them, the One to whom they gave their lives, and the One who loves them more than anyone.

Billy Joe and I Were a Team As a Family and in Ministry

Of course, those of us who love our family member here on earth have mixed feelings. I felt the shock of no longer having my husband here with me. Billy Joe had been my closest friend, my marriage partner and love for thirty-six years; the father of my children who always seemed to have the right words to say to them as they were growing up. He was my pastor and the pastor of a large congregation who loved him dearly and believed in him. He and I had been a ministry team together as a couple for thirty-six years. Even before we married, we both knew God had called us to ministry together.

Billy Joe also functioned in an apostolic role in the body of Christ—raising up schools, sending out graduates, planting churches, doing mission outreaches locally and globally, and supporting missionaries around the world (many with churches, schools, orphanages, and rescue homes). He was a pastor to pastors and a natural born leader. He was a bridge builder in that he sought to unite ministries and church denominations around the lordship of Jesus Christ and the Great Commission.

He saw the power of television, and he shared the gospel message locally and internationally. In fact, he had just released a new TV series called *360° Life* that had had a major impact on people. Most of all, he was a servant leader in the body of Christ. Even people who didn't go to church were affected by his life in and beyond our community.

I knew the shock that everyone would feel regarding my husband's passing. Once our staff heard the news, our Associate Pastor shared with the congregation. I was told later that, when they heard, they were shocked. Some even stayed to pray for those in the next service. Some walked out not knowing what to think.

Sometimes we become so accustomed to having someone around, thinking that they will always be there, that we are shocked when they are no longer here. We had previously scheduled a special guest speaker at the church that night, and when he heard the news he felt led to have a worship service to allow the Holy Spirit to minister to all the people who gathered to find some comfort for the varied levels of shock they were experiencing.

As our family boarded a plane in Texas to fly back home, we realized how grateful we were that we were together, yet each of us realized that we needed time alone to process everything individually once we arrived.

Billy Joe and I had always done life together. I wasn't expecting things to go in this direction. I remember after releasing him to Jesus and leaving the hospital room, my emotions kicked in. I leaned on a friend and with tears prayed, "Oh, God, help me."

Our family had drawn close to embrace each other as we were guided down a hallway to be alone together in a room just to talk and hug.

It is different when your spouse dies. I suppose that is because you recognize this person who knows you better than anyone, loves you, and has helped you carry life's responsibilities together, and now he or she is suddenly gone. You know you will miss his presence, his love and laughter, his companionship, and his strength. You know that God promises you will see him again, but you know it will be a while.

There's an awareness that you will have to lean upon God even more. It makes the scripture in James 4:14 (NKJV) even more relevant to your heart: "[Life is like] *a vapor that appears for a little time and then vanishes away.*" This is why we should value life and our loved ones while they are here. This doesn't mean we should live in fear or be obsessed with them. It just means we need to be aware of how we relate to those around us. It also means we should not live our lives randomly or aimlessly. God has put us here on earth right now for a purpose. We are not here just to exist. God has a plan for our lives that we learn only through talking with Him and listening to Him through His Word and the still small voice of the Holy Spirit in our hearts. That awareness will cause us to be able to accomplish what we are to do.

Hebrews 9:27 says that every person on earth has an appointed time when he or she will face physical death and pass into eternity. However, I had planned for my husband and I to continue to minister together here on earth until the rapture of the Church. His departure was definitely shocking to my plans.

At the same time I did not feel "shaken" in my relationship with the Lord and my belief in His Word. I certainly didn't understand everything that had happened, but I felt the Holy Spirit urge me not to let my mind be caught up in immediately trying to explain to others why my husband had passed at age 57. God's grace came over me in a very special way.

God brought to my mind Philippians 1:21 (NKJV): "For to me, to live is Christ, and to die is gain." I heard the Lord say, "Sharon, Billy Joe lived out his purpose for Me, and now he has died and gained. However, you are still living here on earth, and your purpose hasn't changed just because he moved from earth to heaven. You still are called and anointed to fulfill My purposes."

Called and Anointed to Finish My Purpose

I felt an assurance within my heart that God was going to guide me and enable me to rise and help lead others forward.

In those next months following, I still had moments when tears would swell in my eyes as I spoke of fond memories, but as quickly as they came, they left. Sometimes others would share a memory with me that would bring the tears, but again, they would seem to subside quickly. I am a tenderhearted person, so tears come easily to me when I'm moved by touching stories.

I must say, however, that I didn't become depressed with grief. Someone gave me a book, *Good Grief,* regarding grief. I know that people respond in various ways when a loved one passes. As I read the book, I didn't relate to many parts of it personally until I read something that seemed to jump out at me.

The author, Granger Westberg, wrote:

> People of faith do not just suddenly get that way. Like an athlete who must stay in physical training, these people are always in training for whatever may come at any time... They realize that life will never be the same again, but they begin to sense that there is much in life that can be affirmed....

At the time of great loss people who have a mature faith give evidence of an uncommon relationship with God. The author also wrote:

> I am convinced of the importance of keeping at the task of nurturing one's faith, because I have seen how such people demonstrate greatest under trial.

Conversely, I now have seen even what happens to people who have not taken seriously the necessity of working at their faith when the going was good. These people seem unprepared to handle even the smaller losses, which face all of us from time to time.[1]

I had started my walk with the Lord forty years prior to the day that Billy Joe passed away. I was 16 years old the night I surrendered to Jesus. I remember hearing God's voice clearly in my heart, "I've called you into ministry. Read your Bible daily and pray daily the rest of your life." This was my first draw from heaven. I believe this was when I became awakened to God's voice and calling upon my life.

Before this I had thought the Bible was boring. I was raised in church. My father was a United Methodist pastor my entire life, and my mother was very supportive to him through the years. I had joined the church as a child, but I didn't really know the Lord personally. At this point I said, "Lord, make the Bible interesting seven days in a row, and I'll read it the rest of my life."

When my mom saw me pick up a Bible to read it, she bought me a modern translation called "The Way"—*The Living Bible*. It was great reading because I understood it, and it had pictures of teenagers just like me and my friends all through it. God kept His word and made it personal to me as I read it seven days in a row. I continued to read it and study it from then on. At first I read the New Testament, Psalms, and Proverbs. Then later I began to read the Old Testament as well.

---

1 Granger E. Westberg. *Good Grief*, Fortress Press, Minneapolis, MN, 1962, 1971, 1997, 62–63.

I am convinced that over time God's Word not only created my view of life, but also gave me counsel, strength, stability, and an assurance that cannot be taken from me.

I remember one day when I was about thirty years of age I was reading my Bible and I thought, "God, is anything happening in me? I'm studying Your Word each day, and I'm confessing scriptures in prayer each day. However, I'm not necessarily in demand as a speaker anywhere."

I heard the Lord say to me, "I am producing stability in you for the future." God began opening doors of "one-on-one" discipleship ministry to me in those early years, speaking at times to groups of people, but more than anything He wanted to work in me personally.

When my husband passed, I felt God's Word rise within me, making me steady and calming my emotions. Scriptures began to come to me that were just what I needed at the time. Those scriptures that I had deposited in my heart and mind over the years began to speak to me.

I Meditated on "Shocked" and "Shaken"

Over the next days and weeks, I meditated on the words *shocked* and *shaken*. When I looked in the dictionary, I was amazed at the differences between these two words.

To be shocked is to experience a sudden violent blow, a sudden disturbance of mind and emotions as through great loss or surprise.[2] I definitely had experienced a blow and a disturbance to my mind and emotions, but I also felt I was still standing, and my relationship with the Lord was still strong.

---

2 *Merriam-Webster's New Collegiate Dictionary,* Third Ed., 1997, 1239.

Then I looked at the word *shaken*. It means to be moved abruptly by force; to become dislodged; to disturb and cause to totter[3] or tremble (with fear); to be at the point of failure or collapse; to stagger or lose determination and strength by a reeling, overwhelming blow which causes a person to vacillate.[4]

I knew that this did not describe me. I didn't get dislodged or vacillate in my relationship with the Lord and His Word. I didn't feel like collapsing. Instead, I wanted to draw to Him and His Word to hear His voice speak to me. I wanted to go to church to be with my church family as well and worship with others around me. This brought me strength and healing in my soul.

Basing Our Faith Upon God's Word

Proverbs 24:10 (AMPC) says, "If you faint in the day of adversity, your strength is small."

I was not shaken from my relationship with Jesus or my faith in His Word. My husband and I had already faced many times of crisis in our lives and had had conversations about keeping faith in God's Word regardless of circumstances.

I could hear words of my husband from the past saying, "Honey, we don't base our faith upon the experiences of others. We base our faith upon God's Word. We don't know everything surrounding the situations people walk through."

Even in our own situation, I thought of various factors along the way that probably didn't help my husband's healing process. I also

---

3 Ibid., 1413.
4 Ibid., 1232.

thought about the book my husband had written earlier, *God Is Not Your Problem.* He gave many insights, helping people to not blame God but to draw to God for help.

When we don't know answers to questions right at the moment, we have to trust that, in time, God will reveal what we need to understand. I will talk about this in later chapters. We have to understand the times we are living in and how our world is being affected by it all.

Hebrews 12:28 (ESV) says, "Let us be grateful for receiving a kingdom that cannot be shaken...." This scripture came to mind and gave me a determination that I could rise up and help others around me to rise up to do all that God had called us to do.

More than anything, our enemy, Satan, wants to stop us in all that we are doing to advance God's Kingdom. We have been given the overcoming power of Jesus Christ living within us. In difficult times Jesus wants to rise up within us to show the enemy that he cannot defeat us or stop us from God's purposes and plans.

A Vision from God

A few days after Billy Joe passed, God gave me a vision of a hammer hitting a bubble, and I heard the Lord say, "The devil came with a hit and thought he could paralyze you, your family, and the vision of Victory." Then I saw hundreds of little bubbles going out from that bubble in every direction, and I heard the Lord say, "But this thing is about to multiply."

"Rise Up and Steady the Ship"

I heard the Lord say, "You've got to rise up and steady the ship to take it forward." I knew people were accustomed to seeing me alongside Billy Joe as a ministry team, and I felt God's assurance that He would enable me to do whatever He said.

When I heard the Lord say, "You've got to rise up and steady the ship," I knew it was a huge ship with many facets—the vision being victory and the vision of Victory.

God's Vision Through Billy Joe for Victory Christian Center

Billy Joe had received God's vision and direction through the years as Victory Christian Center was birthed out of another church. We started pastoring an already-existing church in 1979 that grew from 300 to 2,000 in eighteen months. The board of the church felt we should birth a new church and they would keep the already-existing church in a smaller capacity. We started Victory Christian Center in 1981 with 1,600 people. Years later, we had grown to over 16,000 members. Through God's direction and grace, we had raised up:

- Victory Christian School (K–12 grades started in 1979)
- Victory Bible College (started in 1979)
- Victory Fellowship of Ministries (started in 1980)
- International Victory Bible Institutes around the world (today as of 2016 having more than 1,820 institutes in over 96 countries and 127 IVBIs in U.S. prisons and other countries)

- Camp Victory on 100 acres at Lake Keystone (started in 1989, prayer and missions camp for all ages)
- Victory Kids' Bus Outreach which has evolved into Mobile Kids' Clubs and trucks that travel to neighborhoods all around the city
- The Tulsa Dream Center (opened 2001, feeding thousands and ministering weekly to people spiritually, medically, offering counseling services, tutoring programs, and sports programs)
- Various small relational groups called "Connect Groups"
- "Victory in Jesus," local and international Internet, television, and radio ministry broadcasts
- Other outreaches such as weekly street, jail, and prison ministry.

I prayed, "Lord, You are our stability in the midst of unstable times. Help us stabilize the ship and move it forward."

Worship Opens the Treasure of God's Presence

I remembered Isaiah 33:6 (AMPC), "And there shall be stability in your times, an abundance of salvation, wisdom, and knowledge; the reverent fear and worship of the Lord is your treasure and His." Stability starts with understanding the fear of the Lord—not being afraid of God because He loves each of us—but recognizing our humanness and our dependency upon Him. Our society has lost an understanding of "the fear of the Lord." The fear of the Lord is to keep a consciousness of God's presence, to love Him, and to recognize

His lordship over our lives. Again, it's not about being afraid of God, but having a respect for God by honoring Him with our lives and acknowledging Him to direct our lives. It's recognizing the boundaries and the voice speaking to our thoughts to help us as we live here on earth. "He will be the sure foundation for your times, a rich store of salvation and wisdom and knowledge; the fear of the LORD is the key to this treasure" (Isaiah 33:6, NIV).

Then He says that worshiping the Lord is our treasure. When we worship, we open the treasure of God's presence into our lives. He is able to supply what we need.

I needed wisdom and knowledge and all that the Lord had to give me.

As our congregation worshipped after my husband's passing, the Lord began to supply healing to us as a corporate body. I reflect back particularly on several Sunday night services where we simply worshipped. This is an adjustment for some people because many are so accustomed to having someone preach a message at some point. As we worshipped during this time, the Holy Spirit worked His message of healing in our souls.

The knowledge of God's Word gives us wisdom. Proverbs 4:5 (AMP) says, "Get [skillful and godly] wisdom! Acquire understanding [actively seek spiritual discernment, mature comprehension, and logical interpretation]! Do not forget nor turn away from the words of my mouth."

I also needed wisdom and knowledge in practical areas of leadership. I read books, but I felt I was learning more from listening to those around me. I am grateful for trustworthy and faithful men who had served with my husband and who understood what we needed and were able to give counsel to me at that time.

I spent time each week listening to the Lord for His messages for our congregation to be strengthened. There were decisions to be made that I had to hear from the Lord. Some were not easy.

It was a testing time, but God surrounded us as a church with a special grace that produced stability in us as a church body. There were some who left because they told me they just couldn't stand not seeing my husband in the pulpit. I felt that had they stayed long enough to let the Holy Spirit heal them, it would have benefitted them in going forward in their walk with the Lord. However, they did what they felt to do.

The Holy Spirit Often Functions As a "Shock Absorber"

The Holy Spirit is a "shock absorber." We felt the Holy Spirit taking the shock away and guiding us forward.

When we face sudden tests in our lives, the Holy Spirit is like a shock absorber. I thought about how cars have shock absorbers that enable them to drive over rough terrain without the car violently shaking. Shock absorbers absorb shock so the car drives much smoother than it would have. I also thought about other types of transportation. For example, ships have a device called a "stabilizer," which enables them to steadily go through rough, troubled waters and remain intact, not breaking down.

The Holy Spirit is our stabilizer. He keeps us steadily going forward right in the middle of troubled times. We experienced this firsthand as a staff and congregation. It was all of us being determined to follow God and His wisdom, working together as a team.

Stronger Together!

I watched as many took a sense of responsibility and rose up to lead along with me. It reaffirmed the vision of the hammer hitting the bubble that the Lord had showed me. Just like that bubble multiplying into hundreds of bubbles going in all directions, people around me rose to God's calling. Sometimes people can become too dependent on one person to do everything. I watched God spread out the responsibility among us. We each grew stronger.

I've heard it said when a broken bone heals it can become stronger than some of the other bones. We definitely became stronger together. I believe it was because we had to lean on the Lord more than ever. Sometimes growth is forced upon us. However, we make the choice to grow or not to grow.

Ephesians 6:10 (NKJV) says, "Be strong in the Lord and in the power of His might." Many times we learn to do things in our own strength. When we feel pressured to rely upon the Lord more, He supplies something supernatural to us, and it ends up bringing Him glory.

Chapter 2

WHAT
HAPPENED?

IT IS IMPORTANT FOR each of us to know that our purpose in living on earth is much higher than our human minds can imagine. Once you and I surrender our lives to the Lord, He desires to unfold His will to us. Jesus, in fact, told us to pray, "Your will [Lord] be done on earth as it is in heaven" (Matthew 6:10, NKJV). God's will is always going to be about connecting us with others so His plans and purposes can be fulfilled in the earth.

Through the years God called Billy Joe and me to not only pastor a local congregation, but also to reach people around the world with the gospel. My husband heard from the Lord (from heaven) various ways we could multiply God's Word in other nations.

One of these ways was to establish International Bible Institutes throughout the world. We had first established our base here—Victory Bible College, and with it, our missions training center. Through Victory Bible College we sent missionaries to the nations, both in short-term mission work and also raising up long-term mission bases in various nations. Many have established churches, orphanages, International Bible Institutes, Christian schools, and evangelistic teams going into prisons and jails. We connected with other ministries as well as in evangelism and humanitarian aid.

Billy Joe and I would go to places and hold week-long crusade outreaches, teach pastors and leaders, and hold a Women's Conference. We brought humanitarian aid and then started the Bible Institute.

In the summer of 2008, Billy Joe and I had gone to Kigali, Rwanda, Africa, to hold a special evangelistic outreach there in the capital city with nightly large mass gatherings. Along with this we would be doing a Leadership/Pastors' Conference each day and a Women's Conference. Flying overseas, especially into South and Central Africa, is a very lengthy and exhausting flight. However, my husband had been pushing himself prior to this trip and had developed what appeared to be flu-like symptoms, so by the time we landed he was red hot with fever. The glands of his neck were swollen on the right side, and he was extremely tired. He rested the first day before the meetings began, and he turned the daytime Leadership/Pastors' Conference over to me and to other team members so he could preserve his strength for the night meetings. Each night he preached to crowds of people in a sports field, many received the Lord, and as he prayed for the sick many were healed.

Through the years, I've always been amazed by how God will use any of the people who are willing to allow Him to, in our weakest times, to minister to others. This is so that we will always know that it's of Him, from Him, to Him, about Him, and all the glory is for Him.

Once we returned to Tulsa, Billy Joe went to see his general doctor who referred him (and me) to a specialist. The specialist greeted us and said, "Do you remember me?" My husband said, "I'm not sure."

He then went on to tell us how twenty-one years earlier, in 1989, he had been called to a local hospital on an occasion when my husband had become very ill. At that time, the glands on both sides of Billy Joe's neck were swollen, and doctors could not agree on the diagnosis of his condition.

One doctor thought Billy Joe had an extreme case of mononucleosis, an infectious disease. However, another doctor thought he had a rare disease called chronic lymphocytic leukemia. At that time, only a few people in the entire United States had been diagnosed with this illness, and no cure or effective treatment had yet been discovered to treat it.

On the third day in his hospital room, Billy Joe told me that he felt the presence of God fill the room, and he sensed he was healed of whatever the illness was. Then he felt that God led him to take a two-month rest at home. He changed his diet during this time as well, and he regained his strength. He was out of the pulpit for three weeks, and then returned preaching on the weekends again.

Billy Joe began to meet with his staff at our home each week over the next four to five months and eventually returned to his normal office schedule.

For the next 21 years, he was careful to exercise and protect his health. He only had flu symptoms a few times. Whenever he was ill, usually the glands would start to swell. He would rest a day or two, pray Scripture, sometimes fast and pray, get on an antibiotic, and the glands would return to normal.

As the specialist spoke with us, he said he felt his original diagnosis back in 1989 had been correct. He shared with us that over the years a treatment had been developed that they called a miracle drug, because it had been very effective with the majority of patients who had experienced this disease.

He scheduled my husband for the first treatment at a clinic in our city that November. Afterward it seemed that the doctor was right in that the glands in my husband's neck reduced to normal. His white count became normal, and he felt better than he had in a long time.

A few months later, just before he was scheduled for the second treatment, his glands started to swell slightly again, but this subsided after the second treatment. Again his white count was normal, and he felt good.

The specialist felt that he should be examined at an out-of-state hospital, which specialized in this disease, just to make sure everything was going well or if we needed to do something else. At the time Billy Joe felt good and didn't feel he needed to go to the other hospital.

As we came to the third month after the treatment, my husband's schedule picked up again. The glands began to swell, and he felt tired. Our annual Word Explosion week of meetings day and night came at this time with guest speakers for eight days straight. Along with this, many of our missionaries and the ministers in our fellowship of churches came in from around the world to meet. We also were conducting board meetings regarding our plans for the upcoming year with all of our schools, missions, and outreaches.

When the week finally ended, Billy Joe was exhausted. We attempted to schedule an appointment with the out-of-state specialized hospital, but they were booked and could not see Billy Joe for three weeks. During this time a doctor gave him some prednisone to bring down the swelling of the glands.

Finally, we traveled to an out-of-state hospital to meet with the disease specialist there. He shared that it was slightly hard to determine Billy Joe's true condition since the prednisone was in his system, but he felt very good about a treatment that they had that could eradicate the disease. Although the prednisone had reduced the swelling of the glands, it had left his immune system weakened.

About that same time, an infection developed in Billy Joe's throat and his first thought was that it was strep throat. When the medicine for strep throat was completely ineffective, he was already scheduled to see the local disease specialist who examined him and saw that he was dehydrated and quickly hooked him up to some fluids. The specialist realized it was a viral infection and immediately admitted him to a local hospital. This was when the disease transformed from chronic lymphocytic leukemia into an aggressive type of lymphoma cancer.

Billy Joe had been very emphatic about not sharing his condition up until this point. Some people later challenged me on this. I tried to explain that my husband was always very aware that people like to speak their opinions on things, which may not be for the good of someone else. Those who speak negatively do not help someone who is believing for a miracle and speaking their faith. He believed Proverbs 18:21 that "death and life are in the power of the tongue..." and that we eat the fruit of our words. He was very guarded with his words and wanted me and others to be guarded with our words as well. I respected him for this.

At this time, one of our doctor friends advised that Billy Joe write a statement to be read to our congregation since he would be out of the pulpit for the next two weeks. In the statement, Billy Joe asked for people to pray, assuring them that we were pursuing a treatment that had had good results with patients. People began to contact us from everywhere that they were praying in agreement with us for his healing. Our prayer ministry at Victory began to pray a collection of healing scriptures that I sent to them, so we would all be in agreement for the miracle we were confident would come.

Billy Joe Starts Treatment Program at Out-of-State Hospital

After some time in the local hospital, my husband was strong enough to begin the treatment program he had signed up for at the hospital out of state. That hospital was in the midst of an expansion and remodeling project because they needed more rooms. We came to a quick understanding of their need when it took a full eight hours before finally getting Billy Joe into a room. He started the treatment, and very soon, it appeared that the cancer cells were dying and new bone marrow was being produced. Billy Joe had also been determined that he was going to perform the wedding of our youngest son, Paul, and his fiancée, Ashley, that weekend.

Billy Joe's Last Service: Performing Paul and Ashley's Wedding

Resting for one day after the treatment was finished, we returned home. That weekend Billy Joe performed the wedding with the help of one of our assistant pastors. That turned out to be the last service he was able to be a part of. Of course, there was a huge crowd on hand to see and hear him, and you can imagine, I'm sure, how emotional the wedding was for everyone, including me and our family.

Billy Joe Strong in Faith for His Healing

After the wedding, Billy Joe's faith was strong for his healing. I had seen him rise up many times in the past and overcome various circumstances with his faith, and I believed he would rise up out of this as well.

Over the next few weeks, we were in and out of the hospital here in our city. Another infection set in, and other cancer cells appeared in another part of his body. It seemed that his body was weakening. He was scheduled to go back for another treatment at the out-of-state hospital.

Our local hospital had been very loving and caring. They had not wanted to release Billy Joe until they could be assured that he would be transported immediately into a hospital room with all the medical provisions he required. It seemed one moment we were promised that there was a room and the next moment we wouldn't know if a room was available. Although we were uneasy about it, we were told that they had the treatment he needed, and we needed to go.

Our local hospital air-flighted us to the other hospital, and, upon arrival, we were placed in a private room immediately, but we had to wait to be transferred to the floor where Billy Joe needed to be. I handed all of my husband's records to the nurse on duty. When the doctor arrived and asked for the records, I told him I had given them to the nurse, but no one could find them. He then said I would have to write all of my husband's medical history again for them.

I tried so hard to remember it all, but had to call our friend at the hospital back home who was a head nurse. She quickly made copies of what they had and resent them. A day later the out-of-state hospital found the original records which had been misplaced by the nurse.

The hospital felt they needed to wait for my husband to regain some strength before starting the next treatment, but instead of regaining strength, his body weakened.

In those final days before Billy Joe passed, he had many medical tubes hooked up to him and could not communicate. We surrounded him with our prayers and read the Word of God along with worship. Various ministry friends came and prayed for him as well. I'm so thankful for the support of the family of God.

Right before Billy Joe passed, I remembered that Brother Oral Roberts had told me to call him in order to keep him aware of Billy Joe's condition, so I called Brother Roberts. He had always loved Billy Joe like a son, and I knew he would be able to say a prayer of healing and faith, standing with me to rebuke the sickness and the spirit of death from his body.

When I called Brother Roberts' number, his private nurse answered my call, and I explained the situation to her. She, in turn, explained the situation to Brother Roberts since he had become slightly hard of hearing. I didn't want to have to yell over the phone to him since we were in a hospital with other patients in rooms nearby.

Brother Roberts got on the phone and began to pray:

"Billy Joe, I love you so much. You're like a son to me. I release you to go home, and I'll see you soon."

What? I thought. *He doesn't understand.* I wanted him to pray a prayer of healing, not release Billy Joe to go to heaven. But I told Brother Roberts "thank you" and hung up the phone, questioning in my mind why he had said what he did and having thoughts of not wanting Billy Joe to leave.

Later, I called another ministry friend to pray for resurrection. Two hours later Billy Joe passed. Hebrews 11:35 tells us that when a Christian dies, they obtain a better resurrection.

Looking back now, I find it interesting how Brother Roberts was aware of something that I was not aware of at that moment. He spoke his love to Billy Joe in the phone call, and barely three weeks later on December 15, 2009, Brother Roberts joined him in heaven. They did, in fact, "see each other soon."

Our family felt we were to be involved in speaking and singing at Billy Joe's memorial service, along with ministry friends who shared. Over 10,000 people attended the service held in the ORU Mabee Center. Some watched by live stream across the street at our sanctuary. I was amazed at so many ministers and people who came from around the world in honor of Billy Joe's life. The Trinity Broadcasting Network (TBN) aired the service, which lasted about four hours.

Congressmen and Senators who had been touched by Billy Joe's life were there. Oklahoma Senator Jim Inhofe took time the following day to talk about it on the floor of Congress in Washington, DC.

Christians from various denominations were present. Jewish friends from our community were present because of Billy Joe's involvement with Christians United for Israel. Hundreds of pastors came, along with missionaries from other countries.

The powerful presence of God filled the building, and we shared Billy Joe's favorite video called, "The Harvest." This short film features a farm family whose father has passed away, leaving fields of wheat that needed to be harvested or be lost. The wife and young sons prayed, and one morning huge combines came from everywhere. The combines were driven by other farmers coming to help that family bring in the harvest from their fields.

We cried every time we watched this video. Our son, Paul, leaned over to me and said, "Mom, we're the farm family, and there are other farmers here today." I knew in my spirit that together we are all going to bring in the harvest.

We had asked our friend in ministry, John Bevere, to conclude the memorial service with an invitation to hear the call of God and respond that day. He ended by sharing John 12:24–26 (AMP):

> I assure you and most solemnly say to you, unless a grain of wheat falls into the earth and dies, it remains alone [just one grain, never more]. But if it dies, it produces much grain and yields a harvest. The one who loves his life [eventually] loses it [through death], but the one who hates his life in this world [and is concerned with pleasing God] will keep it for life eternal. If anyone serves Me, he must [continue to faithfully] follow Me [without hesitation, holding steadfastly to Me, conforming to My example in living and, if need be, suffering or perhaps dying because of faith in Me]; and wherever I am [in heaven's glory], there will My servant be also. If anyone serves Me, the Father will honor him.

Many responded to the call of God that day to reach beyond themselves and to allow God to use their lives for His purposes from that day on.

Just a few weeks after Billy Joe's death, my father, a retired Methodist pastor who was 91 years old, also passed away. Months before, he had expressed that he was ready to go to heaven, and we had known he was going to pass soon. Still, this brought another change in our family's lives in a matter of just a few weeks. We stayed together through these weeks, and it gave strength to all of us. My brother and I officiated at my dad's funeral. Our family was very aware of how things can suddenly change and how important it is to live for eternity.

Angel Escort Into Eternity

It's important for us to recognize that angels are involved around our lives at all times. Angels are spirit beings from God. They are watchers sent to carry out the will of God on earth (see Daniel 4:13). The Hebrew word for "angel" is *malak,* meaning to dispatch as a deputy from God; a messenger; an ambassador. Hebrews 1:14 (AMPC) says, "Are not the angels all ministering spirits (servants) sent out in the service [of God for the assistance] of those who are to inherit salvation?"

I believe angels were present that morning when my husband slipped into eternity. As I shared earlier, I heard many singing with me from a distance as I worshipped next to Billy Joe's body. I also believe, according to Scripture, that at the death of a believer who has given his life to Jesus, angels assist his passing into heaven (see Luke 16:22).

Jesus said that He has prepared a place for us in heaven and that He receives us to Himself when we die (see John 14:2–3). Notice that

He doesn't *take* us; He *receives* us as we pass into eternity. We return to where we came from.

I've read testimonies of people who have had out-of-body experiences where they left their body after an accident and went to heaven and then returned. They said spirit beings were with them ascending up to heaven. When they arrived, they felt as if they were home.

Friend, heaven is our ultimate home, and we are headed there. We will be joined with others there who have gone on before us. Until that time, while we are here on earth, we are not on our own. God wants us to recognize that angels are here to help us; and as we call upon heaven's help and speak His Word, angels will continue to help us in the days ahead.

Chapter 3

WHY?

(COMMON QUESTIONS AT THE UNEXPECTED PASSING OF A LOVED ONE)

T HE QUESTIONS COME TO mind, "What about all the prayers that were being prayed? Why did Billy Joe die when he was having such an impact upon the world?" I do not claim to have all the answers, but I do feel that I have some insights that have helped me.

A few years before Billy Joe passed, he wrote an excellent book titled *God Is Not Your Problem*. He felt that through the years many people have blamed God for allowing, permitting, or giving access to tragedy in their lives. I believe it's important that we not see God as our problem but as our answer so that instead of drawing away from Him at the death of a loved one, we draw to Him because He is the only One who can meet the deepest needs in our lives.

1. First of all, we need to realize that we have an enemy: Satan.

In John 10:10 (GNT), Jesus called Satan a thief. He said, "The thief comes only in order to steal, kill, and destroy. I have come in order that you might have life—life in all its fullness." Satan seeks to take life, while Jesus gives life. Satan has demonic spirits who seek to carry out his attacks.

Paul wrote in Ephesians 6:12 (NKJV), "For we do not wrestle against flesh and blood, but against principalities, against powers, against the rulers of the darkness of this age, against spiritual hosts of wickedness in the heavenly places." This scripture speaks of Satan's demonic spirits who seek to come against us while we are here on earth. Many Christians act as if there is no battle going on around them. Instead, they live carelessly and without wisdom, thinking they are okay when, in reality, they are surrounded by an enemy who is against them.

Years ago, after the Columbine High School shooting in Littleton, Colorado, Billy Graham was interviewed about the tragedy on the *Larry King Live* television show. Larry King asked him, "Reverend Graham, how do you explain this?" Without hesitating, Billy Graham said, "There are demons in the earth. They cause things to happen that are not rational."

I remember when, years ago, a man came to our church who seemed very anxious throughout the service. When my husband gave the invitation, he came up and hit my husband with his fist, leaving a cut above my husband's eye, which required stitches afterward. Then he hit two other gentlemen as several men attempted to carry him out. One of the men he hit was an officer, who put the troubled man in jail. When my husband went to the jail to visit him, his speech and demeanor seemed to be off kilter. Something was just not right. He had a list of ministers that he had planned to hit. He had been living in a mental institution but had been released briefly. After this he was sent back to a mental institution.

One year later, he wrote my husband and said, "I don't know if you will remember me, but I came to your church, and I hit you one Sunday. I don't know what came over me to do that. Will you pray for me that I will never do that again?"

Of course, we knew what had come over him to do that—a demonic spirit. We prayed for him and discovered that other Christians had gone to minister to him. The point is, demonic spirits are operating in the world around us.

In January 2008, my husband and I were praying together about the new year, and he turned to me and said, "I get inside of my spirit that everything is about to intensify." Little did we realize that the following year we would be walking through a physical attack of the enemy against my husband's body.

Over the past few years, I've seen many other believers pass into eternity. None of those who have passed were defeated because Jesus told us, "I am the resurrection and the life. He who believes in Me, though he may die, he shall live. And whoever lives and believes in Me shall never die…" (John 11:25–26, NKJV).

Those who have believed and received Jesus as Lord and Savior here on earth never die. At physical death, we cease existing in a mortal body, but our spirit and soul continue to exist as we go to heaven. There we receive wholeness and a glorified body that is very real. (See Luke 24:36-43.) Everything is beautiful there. There are no more battles. There is victory and fullness of life in every way.

We need to be aware that there is a battle here on earth as long as we are here. Revelation 12:12 tells us that the devil comes down (from the heavenly realm around us) with great wrath because he knows that his time is short. Satan knows he has a certain amount of time to be loosed in the earth before he will be bound for a thousand years.

Remember in Matthew 8:29 when the demons said to Jesus, "Have You come here to torment us before the time?" (NKJV). The demonic spirits know they have a period of time on earth, so they have increased their activity in these last days. As believers, we cannot have a casual attitude about our enemy. *Whether we want to be at war or not, we have an enemy who knows he is at war with us.*

This is why we pray. This is why we study God's Word: so we know how to handle it like a weapon. This is why we worship, because worship binds the enemy. This is why we stay in a life-giving church with other believers because we know we need the family of God around us. We can't fight alone. This is why we listen to the teaching of God's Word, so we are sharpened in our discernment of the enemy. (See Ephesians 6:10–18, NKJV.) God has said that He has given us weapons of warfare against the enemy and we have to learn our weapons and use them (2 Corinthians 10:3–6).

2. We need to realize we live in a fallen world.

Because of Adam and Eve's sin, they opened up the world to sin and death. This includes sickness and disease, calamities, abuse, tragedies, sin, and every form of evil around us in this world.

Before the fall, God had created everything good and perfect (see Genesis 1:31). There was no evil or knowledge of evil. God had placed the tree of the knowledge of good and evil in the Garden because He wanted Adam and Eve to choose to love and obey Him. He did not create them to be robots. He gave them freedom of choice to choose.

He warned them not to choose to eat of the one tree because it would bring death. God gives every person freedom to choose. It's called free will.

The world we live in is still under the influence of the enemy. Satan has the ability to operate with his demonic spirits in our world. God owns the earth and everything in it, but Satan has access in it at this time. (See Psalm 89:11; 2 Corinthians 4:4; Ephesians 2:2.)

You may say, "Well, I thought Jesus defeated the devil on the cross and when He was raised from the dead." Colossians 2:14–15 tells us that Jesus "spoiled principalities and powers" and put Satan to shame. Jesus took the keys of death, hell, and the grave (see Revelation 1:18), and then He took back the authority that Satan had held over people (see Colossians 1:13). Once we are saved, we have to know we can use the authority Jesus gave us through His name and enforce Satan's defeat using God's Word. Then we have to listen to Jesus' leading while we are walking about in this world. It's similar to wartime where an enemy has left explosives around that are still operative and can injure and kill.

I remember while visiting in Israel one time, we came to an area where our guide explained that the people who lived nearby knew they could not casually go for a walk out in a certain field, because old explosive traps were still there that could go off and kill whoever came upon them.

The Holy Spirit in the Word of God has been given to us to help us discern things around us.

3. Realize we are living in the last days.

A ministry friend, who has been one of my spiritual coverings since my husband passed, sent me an insight that has helped me in regard to the days we are living in.

Rick Renner shares in his book, *Sparkling Gems from the Greek,* that 2 Timothy 3:1 tells us, "But know this, that in the last days perilous times will come" (NKJV). This word *perilous* is the Greek word *chalepos.* This word is only used one other time in Scripture, and that is in Matthew 8:28. Jesus and the disciples had just crossed over the Sea of Galilee having come through a storm caused by an underwater earthquake. They arrived at the land of Gergesenes, and two demon-possessed men came out of the tombs who were "exceedingly fierce." These two words, "exceedingly fierce," are the Greek word *chalepos.*

Chalepos has the meaning of being wild, vicious, unpredictable, and uncontrollable like a wild animal. It means these end times are dangerous times that are high risk and can be harmful. We are living in times of great stress where words will be spoken around us that are difficult and emotionally hard to bear. All of this describes the signs of the times that we have entered into.

We all have heard negative words at times, whether from a doctor's report or from listening to the news, or maybe a family member has said something that has stirred you to pray. You may have faced a disappointment suddenly for which you had not prepared. You may be walking through a battle even right now that has tried to create stress in your life. Whatever it is, you are not alone. God is right there with you, and He has wisdom to guide you.

I like the Psalms because David lets us see that no matter what he was facing and walking through, he believed God was for him, that He was with him, and that He would deliver him. (See Psalm 56:3–13, NKJV.)

Things Have Become More Intense

I know you would agree with me that things are different than they were ten years ago, twenty years ago, and forty years ago. Everything has "intensified" as my late husband said. I know I have to be more knowledgeable, more alert, wise, and more discerning than I may have been forty years ago. We all need this.

> *For though we walk in the flesh, we do not war after the flesh:*
> *(For the weapons of our warfare are not carnal, but mighty through God to the pulling down of strong holds;)*
> *Casting down imaginations, and every high thing that exalteth itself against the knowledge of God, and bringing into captivity every thought to the obedience of Christ.*
> —2 CORINTHIANS 10:3–5

One night the week before my husband passed, I had gone home to rest and a friend of ours stayed the night with Billy Joe in the hospital. About 3:00 to 4:00 a.m. Billy Joe woke up and called out to our friend Bruce to help him pray. Bruce came over to the bedside and began praying in the Spirit. Billy Joe told him he had a dream that he was inside a bunkhouse alone and fiery missiles were coming down upon him from every direction. They prayed, and Billy Joe fell back asleep.

Two years later my grandmother died who was 102 years old and very sound-minded. However, before she passed, she had a reoccurring dream three times of fiery missiles coming down on the earth. At first she thought it was an attack on the United States, but when she had the dream again, she said she saw it was coming down on several nations. It disturbed her and she said she had prayed not to have the dream again.

I told her about Billy Joe's dream before he passed and how that I felt she had seen over into the spirit world at the battle that was going on.

4. Sometimes the Holy Spirit attempts to warn us, but we miss the warning.

I've thought of times where I have missed hearing the Holy Spirit. However, I have chosen not to condemn myself over it. I have chosen instead to learn from these times of missing it and learn His ways better. The Holy Spirit will sometimes drop a thought into your heart that you have not been thinking about, and He nudges you to do something or not to do something. Learning how to respond to His thoughts helps us grow in our relationship with Him.

In our humanity, we sometimes miss God's promptings. In Acts 27, we can study the account of Paul who had appealed to speak to Caesar. Along with other prisoners, He was delivered to the care of a centurion and his soldiers to sail on a ship to Italy.

The weather looked fine to begin with, but along the way they ported at an area of Crete. Paul discerned in his spirit that they should not travel after they had spent time in that area. He discerned they would be heading at that point into dangerous weather at sea. The captain, however, was just looking at the present weather conditions and decided they would travel on.

After being at sea a short time, a hurricane came and tossed the ship for fourteen days. It looked like all hope of survival was gone. However, Paul was praying and fasting and an angel appeared to him. The angel assured him that in spite of their missing it in traveling that God was going to save their lives if they stayed with the ship. They did and they were saved.

5. Sometimes we want God to do something a certain way, and He may be doing it another way.

Remember how in 2 Kings 5, Naaman, the captain of the Syrian army, had contracted leprosy. A young girl who worked for him told him about Elisha the prophet who lived in Israel. She knew Elisha had been used by God to heal people. When he went to Elisha's house, he wanted Elisha to come and pray for him to be healed of leprosy, but Elisha sent word from a distance, telling him to go dip in the dirty Jordan River seven times and he would be healed. At first, he didn't want to do it that way. But finally, others talked him into it, and when he obeyed, he was healed (2 Kings 5:10-14).

When you face a negative report, pray and listen to God speak to your thoughts. It's important to pray and hear from God what His plan of action is to be and not limit yourself to one way that you might think it should be. God uses various ways to work in our lives.

6. Sometimes others make mistakes that negatively affect us.

In this case we have to choose to forgive and believe that God will work supernaturally in our lives because we have kept our heart right toward others and toward Him.

A family we knew years ago chose to forgive when a mistake was made in the hospital where their loved one was a patient. That mistake caused tragedy in that family's lives. God gave them great grace, and they have been used by the Lord to minister to others over the years. Had they chosen another course, their ministry and God's plan for them and others might have been forever deterred.

7. Sometimes there are hindrances that we are not aware of in our lives.

However, the Holy Spirit can reveal things to us as we are open to Him.

In the book, *None of These Diseases* by Dr. S. I. McMillen, he helps us see that emotions such as anger, deep hurt, rejection, lust, malice, fear, anxiety, self-centeredness, resentment, lying, and any other negative emotions can aggravate the body's immune system, producing stress and causing disease in a person. Dr. McMillen also brings out practical knowledge about other contributors to disease.

8. Realize there are sometimes factors involved when a person dies that you do not know.

First Corinthians 13:12 (GW) says, "Now we see a blurred image in a mirror. Then we will see very clearly. Now my knowledge is incomplete. Then I will have complete knowledge as God has complete knowledge of me."

When we choose to put our trust in the Lord with what we don't understand at the moment and we continue to seek Him, eventually He will reveal things to us. Sometimes things are kept in God's secret place because He knows what we can handle on earth at the place of spiritual growth where we are. He promises we will know ultimately either on this side of eternity or when we go to heaven to be with Him. The important thing is that we not let the enemy hinder us in continuing to seek the Lord, because that is where our strength is.

Deuteronomy 29:29 says, "The secret things belong unto the LORD our God: but those things which are revealed belong unto us and to our children for ever...."

9. I had various ones give me their thoughts about my husband's passing at the age that he passed.

One person gave me Isaiah 57:1 and said that my husband was taken away from the evil to come. Of course, my thought was, *What about us and others still here?* I thought about it later and became open to the fact that sometimes there are things we don't see ahead, but I believe God gave me peace in knowing that my husband saw into eternity and released himself to enter into that rest.

Another told me that Billy Joe had fulfilled his destiny and appointed time here on earth. I've been open to the Lord regarding the timing of his passing. I know that God was not caught off guard. I also know that each of us as family members have risen in God's strength and calling to do what we might not have done had Billy Joe still been on earth. I think about it now that we leaned upon him a lot. He was a wonderful leader to our family!

Since Billy Joe's passing I have observed that the body of Christ has gone through much transition. There has been the passing of the baton of leadership to the younger generation in many ministries around the world. There is still a role and purpose for all generations, but God has been transitioning people. We are all going to bring in the harvest.

Billy Joe was 57 years old when he passed. Billy Joe's earthly father passed at age 57 from an accident, and he spoke at his father's memorial service.

Billy Joe was driven by his sense of destiny. He loved God and loved people and felt driven to reach everyone he could. He had a sense of responsibility in living his life to the max while on earth. It was hard for him to just take time for himself to rest. I'm grateful for the time I had with him on earth. He died doing what he wanted to do and was fulfilled in that. And that gives me great peace.

Acts 13:36 (NKJV) speaks of David and says, "After he had served his own generation by the will of God, fell asleep, was buried with his fathers...." Billy Joe served his generation, and he imparted vision into the next generation and trained believers to do the work of the ministry—his own family and others. The last two sermons he preached were "Raising up the Next Generation" and "Connecting the Family." That's powerful when I think about it.

Do I believe he fulfilled the number of his days? Well, I know he filled all of his days full. I'm at peace with the life that he lived here on earth. I'm watching our children rise up in their callings and leaning upon the Lord's strength, and I'm grateful.

I've grown deeper and stronger in my walk with the Lord, and Billy Joe's life still inspires me today to have a sense of responsibility to this generation. We are all needed at "such a time as this."

Chapter 4

LIVE FOR JESUS

O NE OF THE FIRST scriptures that I heard in my spirit when Billy Joe passed was Philippians 1:21 (NKJV): "For to me, to live is Christ, and to die is gain." When I had the opportunity to spend time alone with God after that, He reminded me of the beginning of the relationship Billy Joe and I shared, because I was at the same point again of soul-searching in my life.

I heard the Lord say, "Sharon, Billy Joe lived for Me and fulfilled his purpose, and now he has died and he has gained. You are still here living on earth and your purpose hasn't changed. Your purpose is still to live for Me and serve Me in ministry." With this in mind, I want to share with you our story.

Our Story

Billy Joe and I surrendered our lives to Jesus Christ in 1970. We had grown up in church. My father was a United Methodist pastor, and we moved to Magnolia, Arkansas, during the summer of 1969. The following year God brought a spiritual awakening to our church and particularly to our youth group. We became spiritually hungry and radically saved. This awakening was happening among youth from other churches as well. In fact, we discovered later we were a part of what was known as "The Jesus Movement."

Another church in town invited teens from other churches to get involved in a youth musical. One of the nights of that musical I was singing, and I heard the voice of God say to step forward and make a commitment to live for Jesus—to do whatever that involved. I was overwhelmed by the presence of God.

That night I heard the voice of God in my spirit for the first time in a strong way. He spoke to me as I mentioned earlier, "I've settled your salvation. There will be no more doubts. I've called you to ministry. Read your Bible, and pray daily." I prayed, "Lord, when I read it, let it speak to me every day for seven days, and I'll do what You say the rest of my life."

I thought the new paperback Bible called *The Living Bible* that my mother bought for me was awesome! I could understand it, and it had pictures of teenagers throughout. I felt that God was speaking to me every day, and He was. I made a commitment to read it daily the rest of my life.

A few weeks later, Billy Joe graduated from high school, and one day he pulled up to a service station to get gas. A guy who had just graduated from the college in our town was getting gas also, and he said, "Hey, Billy Joe, you just graduated, didn't you?" Then he pulled out his clock radio and said, "I apologize that I don't have a gift for you, but I want to give you my clock radio." Then he told Billy Joe he was headed to serve in the Army. Billy Joe was so touched by his gift because he knew Jim didn't have much and that he didn't have any money to spend either. Tears came to his eyes, and he was a little choked up over Jim's gesture.

Since it was lunchtime, Billy Joe asked Jim to come to his house for lunch. Billy Joe didn't know until he told him later that Jim had prayed for him at a distance for four years while he was in the college in our town.

That day after they ate, Jim asked Billy Joe if he had ever really been born again. Prior to this, Billy Joe had found a little tract called "The Four Spiritual Laws" by Bill Bright of Campus Crusade, and had read it. In fact, Billy Joe had to give an extemporaneous speech in his speech class the last week of school, so he used that little tract to speak from. He said he knew other kids in the class knew he really hadn't ever surrendered to the Lord.

Along with his parents, Billy Joe had grown up going to the Methodist church where my parents were pastoring at that time. Before this, if someone had asked if he knew the Lord, he would have said, "Of course, I'm a Christian." But at that moment when Jim asked him about his true spiritual condition, his heart had been opened to really be honest about his life, and he told Jim no, he hadn't really been born again. At that point, Billy Joe received Jesus into his heart as his Lord and Savior. He surrendered his life and future to God.

He said everything around him changed from that moment on. After this is when we began dating. We both knew we had a call of God upon our lives.

Billy Joe would get up early every morning to read the Word and pray before going to work. Unusual things began happening to him that he didn't tell anyone about for over a year. He had an open vision of the two of us ministering to a mass of people. Being in a church of only about 250 people and being Methodist, we had never experienced seeing a mass of people. He kept that to himself and waited a long time before sharing it with me. We knew nothing about spiritual dreams and visions.

Later, he had another open vision while on a football field and saw on what appeared to be a television screen, people living for one thing after another—to graduate from high school, work, get a car, go to college or get some vocational training, get a job, get married, buy a house, raise a family, get another house and car, send the children to college, see them marry and have kids, retire, get a house on a lake, and die. And when they looked back on their lives, none of the things they accomplished would go into eternity. Then the Lord said, "If you will live for Me, helping people know Me all along the way, one day when you die and step into eternity, all those that you have reached for Me you will take into eternity."

Then the Lord said to Billy Joe, "I'm not saying you won't finish college or you won't get married or have a family, a house, a car, and other things along the way. I'm saying that you won't live for things. You'll live for Me." When Billy Joe shared these visions with me, we knew God had called us together as a team.

I might add that at that time in history, you didn't see husbands and wives in ministry together. Ministry leaders were all men. My parents had worked together in ministry through the years, and my mom was a tremendous support to my dad, but it was my dad who people considered the pastor.

Solidifying Our Spiritual Foundation

Billy Joe and I dated for three years, and were apart from each other part of that time. We became engaged in my junior year and his senior year at Oral Roberts University. Our plan was to be married that summer in August.

We were both very busy with school and work. After we had announced our engagement, one evening Billy Joe asked me to go for a walk with him. He said, "We can't get married."

I was shocked and asked, "Why?" He said, "I've been praying and I feel that our relationship is not what it needs to be; and if we get married now, it could end in a divorce like other Christian couples we know. We need to call off the wedding."

We had bought the engagement ring, and I was wearing it. I had already put my engagement picture and announcement in the paper back home and had begun the preparations for the wedding. I said, "Give me a few days to fast and pray." (I think desperation prompts a person to fast and pray at times, and God moves in their lives to accomplish His will.)

One month before, we had attended a dating, engagement, and marriage seminar held on campus for students. One of the speakers had shared his and his wife's story about how they had broken off their relationship when they went to college and how she almost married someone else. But two weeks before the wedding she called it off, and God led them back together, and they were married. Then he spoke about "trusting God" and how God wants the best for you if you will trust Him with your life.

God brought this back to my mind and said, "Release Billy Joe. Let him go. Do you trust Me that either I will bring him back into your life, or someone better?" Well, at that time I couldn't think of anyone better for my life, but I told the Lord, "Okay, I will trust You."

That weekend I was going on a short ministry trip with a few other students, and Billy Joe was not going. I was asked to sing, and a friend playing guitar for me suggested a song, "I'd Rather Have Jesus." I didn't know the song, so he sang it to me. The words spoke to my heart, and I knew then and know now that this song was a commitment for me and for those I would be singing it to.

I sang it as tears filled my eyes through the song. I know people must have thought I was falling apart. They didn't know that God was doing a sanctifying work in my life. I had let Billy Joe become my focus, and now my focus had gotten back on track. That May 1973 we went our separate ways because of jobs in different towns.

After a few weeks Billy Joe wrote me and asked what God was saying to me. I wrote back, sharing with him something from my devotional time. He wrote again and asked if I would pray about our relationship being back on. Of course, I wrote him back and said "yes." We got married the end of that summer after all.

Trusting the Integrity of God's Word

You may wonder why I'm sharing this. The week my husband passed, the Lord brought this back to my memory and said, "Sharon, will you trust Me with what you don't understand right now? Can you release it to Me, and then trust that over time I will reveal things to you? Will you take steps of faith to obey My voice beyond your feelings?"

As difficult as that may seem, I responded that I would. I told Him, "Yes, I trust You."

This was very important for me to go forward with my life and to help others go forward and believe that God was with us and was still faithful to His Word.

As I look back on my life, something else very important helped me. I was taught to believe the integrity of God's Word and to know that the Word is what the devil seeks to undermine and destroy in people's minds. Why? Because if the devil convinces a person that they can't believe God's Word, then he knows they have no ability to fight him. Then he can come with various thoughts, such as overwhelming grief that doesn't go away, depression, fear, failure, bitterness toward God and others, possibly adding alcohol and drugs to that, or loneliness and isolation.

I'm aware of one woman who had had a loved one pass away whom she had leaned on. She was lonely and began going to the casino every night. She ended up stealing money from her government job and was caught and sent to prison.

I've known of others who turned to alcohol to try to drown their loneliness. The only One who can supply the comfort and peace of mind that we need is Jesus, and He uses His Church to be a place of relationships where people can find the fellowship they need.

The devil's tactics are always to destroy people and other relationships around them. We have to remember, there is a battle going on and that battle has intensified because we are living in the last of the last days. We also know from God's Word that we never are defeated by the enemy if we continue in our faith in God. The reason for this is that whether we live on earth or we pass into eternity in heaven, we still continue to live; and when we get to heaven we are united again with our Father, our Savior, and the family of God.

Chapter 5

TRUST—THE
SECRET PLACE

"Trust in God at all times...."

—Psalm 62:8, GNT

*"Trust in the LORD with all your heart, and lean not on your
own understanding."*

—Proverbs 3:5, NKJV

I BELIEVE THAT TRUST IS the secret place with God. Of course, trust is
built upon the foundation of God's Word. Satan hates this place of
trust, because trust is a heart matter. Satan cannot operate in a heart
that has settled the position of trusting in the Lord. He attempts to
speak into the soulish realm of a person's emotions and thoughts. The
mind is the battlefield. Satan seeks to sow thoughts of doubt toward
God, or he tries to get you stuck in reasoning on what happened and
why.

When someone understands the secret place of trust in God, they
are not shaken by circumstances around them. They take refuge in the
Lord where He provides a steadiness and a peace that passes human
understanding. (See Psalm 46:1.)

To trust in God is to place your confidence in the integrity, strength, ability, and surety of God and His Word. To trust God, you have to let go of what you might not fully understand at the moment.

I remember hearing Corrie ten Boom share how when she was just a young child, she had overheard some people talking and she asked her father about the facts of life. He responded to her innocence, saying, "Corrie, when we ride the train to go on a long trip, who carries your bag?" She replied, "You do, Papa." He then said, "Corrie, will you trust me? I will carry that bag of information for you until you are old enough and strong enough to carry it yourself." She said she felt pressure taken off of her at that time and was at peace.

When we don't have full understanding of situations at times, our place of refuge is to trust in the Lord. When a strong Christian has had others unexpectedly die, people feel pressured to have immediate answers, or they feel they must explain why. Sometimes God simply speaks to our hearts like Corrie ten Boom's father spoke to her: "Trust me to carry this right now, and I will give you understanding as I think you can handle it in the days ahead." The Lord takes the pressure off of us, trying to explain. He gives us time to let our emotions be healed. Then, over time, He speaks to our thoughts to help us understand more.

Because trust is a heart issue, you have to capture your thoughts and bring them captive. (See 2 Corinthians 10:3–5.) Otherwise your thoughts will try to run wild. You bring your thoughts captive by meditating upon God's Word. Then you have to listen to your heart.

When you trust in the Lord, you believe that He loves you. I am so aware of not only how much my husband loved me, but also how much Jesus loves me. That love gives me assurance that He is taking care of me.

When you trust God, you commit your past, present, and future into His hands. Although there are things ahead that you cannot see fully, you know that God can see and that He will guide you and surround you with His shield of favor and protection.

After my husband passed, many people asked, "Why?" Billy Joe was only 57 years old. He had not only fulfilled the vision that God originally gave him, but he had written additional vision for the future.

These same people knew that we had believed God for his healing here on earth and that many around the world had prayed and fasted, believing with us.

The more I've studied the Scriptures, I firmly believe in those last few days that Billy Joe got a glimpse of heaven and went on over into that place of rest and reward. Heaven is beyond our mind's imagination. When we pass over to the other side of eternity, we will understand the "draw" that heaven has on our lives.

Billy Joe was drawn over into eternity by the presence of God. The moment he passed, he was in the presence of God and he was happy and whole. (See 2 Corinthians 5:8.)

When he passed, I knew in part and trusted that God would reveal things to me over time. One day in heaven I will know fully as I am known. The longer I live, the greater peace I have had with things that were not quickly understood back then.

It is "trust" that enables us to stand strong in spite of what we face. There will be times in every believer's life when your faith and trust will be a conscious choice as you are tempted by the enemy to be led by your emotions of disappointment or pain.

A Song in the Night of Trusting God in Time of a Tragedy

Psalm 42:8 (AMP) says, "...in the night His song shall be with me, a prayer to the God of my life." Job 35:10 (ERV) says, "He is the one who gives us songs to sing in the night."

When a loved one dies, it can feel like a night season. God's Word speaks about how that even in the night, however, He can give us a song of hope and assurance of His loving support. I remember songs that came to me during this time—songs out of my spirit and songs I knew such as "See His Glory Come Down," "Savior King," "Hosanna," "Worshiping You," and an old hymn, "'Tis So Sweet." The story of the hymn "'Tis So Sweet" is very touching and encouraging.

"'Tis So Sweet"—The Story

It was written after Louisa Stead experienced the hardship of losing her husband. Louisa had married in 1875, and she and her husband had a daughter named Lily.

One warm summer day in 1882, Louisa, her husband, and their young daughter Lily decided to go to the beach for a picnic. While there, they heard a boy screaming for help. He was drowning in the water. Louisa's husband ran to rescue him, but the boy pulled Mr. Stead and himself under, and both drowned. Louisa and little Lily stood watching helplessly.

After this, Louisa, without a job or a source of income for her daughter, was in great need. Louisa turned to the Scriptures and began to pray for God's guidance and His provision. The next day someone left food at their door. Day by day they began to see God's provision. Not long after this, one night Louisa wrote the words of the hymn, "'Tis So Sweet to Trust in Jesus," a song that continues to be sung today.

"'Tis So Sweet to Trust in Jesus"[5]

'Tis so sweet to trust in Jesus,
and to take him at his word;
just to rest upon his promise,
and to know, "Thus saith the Lord."

Refrain:
    Jesus, Jesus, how I trust him!
    How I've proved him o'er and o'er!
    Jesus, Jesus, precious Jesus!
    O for grace to trust him more!

O how sweet to trust in Jesus,
just to trust his cleansing blood;
and in simple faith to plunge me
neath the healing, cleansing flood! [Refrain]

Yes, 'tis sweet to trust in Jesus,
just from sin and self to cease;
just from Jesus simply taking
life and rest, and joy and peace. [Refrain]

I'm so glad I learned to trust thee,
precious Jesus, Savior, friend;
and I know that thou art with me,
wilt be with me to the end. [Refrain]

---

5 www.hymnary.org/hymn/UMH/462

In spite of Louisa's husband passing, God took care of her and Lily. She was able, by God's grace, to go forward and see God's plan and purpose unfold for her and her daughter's life.

Shortly after the accident, Louisa and Lily moved to Africa to follow God's call as missionaries. Louisa remarried, and because she did not allow herself to become stuck in grief, many people were reached and influenced by her life. Her daughter Lily continued as a missionary in Africa the rest of her life as well.

Louisa's trust in the Lord created a song that has impacted the lives of thousands of people and has continued to be sung over the past hundred years. This hymn expresses a heart of simple trust in God's Word to meet our every need and an awareness of God's presence continually abiding with us forever.[6]

Results of Choosing to Trust in God and in His Word

What happens when we choose to "trust" in God and in His Word, even when we don't understand everything?

1. We see God's handwork in amazing ways to provide and make a way for our lives as we follow His direction.

2. We impact the lives of others who are watching us, even future generations.

3. God is able to do great things through our lives that we could never do on our own.

---

6 http://www.umcdiscipleship.org/resources/history-of-hymns
-tis-so-sweet-to-trust-in-jesus

4. We conquer and frustrate the enemy because we didn't allow him to defeat us.

5. We grow stronger.

"Trust" Comes Out of Relationship

Trust is something that happens out of relationship. The longer you walk in close relationship with someone, the more you trust them. The longer you walk in close relationship with God, the more you trust Him, even when you can't see what He sees. Relationship, of course, starts with surrender and commitment when you first receive Jesus as Lord and Savior.

Then relationship grows through communication. Reading God's Word is like Him talking to you. Prayer is how you talk to Him and you listen to your heart for Him to talk to you. Prayer is a heart-to-heart relationship with God. It's not just saying some words mechanically. Sometimes you will pray Scripture declaring your faith in His promises. Sometimes you will pray with supplication or asking God for something. Sometimes you will "pray in the Spirit" or in other tongues because the words in your known language just don't seem to come.

Prayer is our communication line with the Lord. Prayer is like breathing. We don't stop breathing when a loved one dies. We don't stop praying either. God responds to us by speaking thoughts to our heart.

When Louisa Stead prayed and read her Bible, thoughts began to come into her heart so she wrote them on paper. Those thoughts from God—which became the hymn, "'Tis So Sweet to Trust in

Jesus"—not only strengthened her, but through the years have strengthened believers around the world.

I, myself, experienced God's inspiration after my husband died, and I wrote a song that I had started writing the year before but had put it aside. The words came back to me, "We Overcome," along with a verse that came during the weeks following my husband's passing:

"We Overcome"

Chorus:
We overcome by the blood of the Lamb.
Oh, we overcome by the blood of the Lamb.
By the word of our testimony we will stand.
Loving Jesus more and more, we'll overcome.

Verse:
Through the fire, through the flame,
Through the waters we've been saved.
Knocked down, we get up again,
'Cuz we've chosen to believe,
And we've chosen we will stand.

(Repeat)

"Made by God for God"

A friend of ours, Rick Renner, has said, "You were made by God and for God, and until you understand that, life will never make sense." My husband and I settled that when we got married that we belonged to God and that we were created for His purposes. The longer we lived and pursued our relationship with God, I believe the more that truth became embedded in our hearts.

My husband would always remind me through the years that no matter what we faced in life, God could turn and work things for good if we would believe and keep our focus on Him. Trusting in God is a choice we make. It is not hard to choose trusting in Him when you realize who your enemy is and that God is the One who is for you, with you, and in you to help you overcome.

In Christ, You'll Not Be Shaken or Moved

Psalm 125:1 (GNT) says, "Those who trust in the LORD are like Mount Zion, which can never be shaken, never be moved."

When we trust in the Lord and in His Word, we are told that we will not be shaken or moved by the storms of life. We are firmly and deeply rooted in our relationship with God. We are told that storms will come in the world that we live in, but when we build our lives doing what God's Word has said, then we have a foundation of faith and trust that will not be shaken or destroyed.

The psalmist said that we have an assurance that the Lord surrounds us like the mountains surround Jerusalem, and those mountains will not be removed. (See Psalm 125:2.) Luke 6:47–49 (MEV) says:

> Whoever comes to Me and hears My words and does them, I will show whom he is like: He is like a man who built a house, and dug deep, and laid the foundation on rock. When the flood arose, the stream beat vehemently against that house, but could not shake it, for it was founded on rock. But he who hears and does not obey is like a man who built a house on the ground without a foundation, against which the stream beat vehemently. Immediately it fell, and the ruin of that house was great.

Once we receive Jesus, we have received the chief cornerstone of our house. From there we choose to begin building the foundation of our lives as we develop our relationship with Him and put His Word in our hearts, praying, being connected with the church, and obeying His voice. This creates a deep and firm foundation.

However, if we choose to go our own way and make it a practice to live according to the desires of our flesh, choosing the easy path that is comfortable with no responsibility, one day a storm or test will hit. When it does, the house will not stand.

The Lord wants to surround us and empower us to overcome in this world that we live in, but He has given us a free will. We can choose to obey Him or not obey His Word.

If you have experienced a shaking in your life, I want to assure you that there is still hope and mercy with the Lord. When you turn to Him and seek Him, He promises to restore and help you rebuild your life.

Heaven is drawn to those who draw to the Lord in faith and trust. He will keep us and He will guide us in the days ahead. He will protect and deliver us because we choose to trust in Him. He will be our Source in every realm of life as we listen to His voice and follow His lead.

The Importance of Waiting Upon the Lord

> *My soul waits calmly for God alone. My salvation comes from him. He alone is my rock and my savior—my stronghold. I cannot be severely shaken.*
>
> —PSALM 62:1–2, GW

In our Western society, there is a busyness that can come easily into anyone's life in a subtle way to distract people from what is vitally important.

People multitask and feel good about accomplishing much in small segments of time. However, there is one thing we cannot multi-task and expect to benefit our lives, and that is *spending quality time with God.*

Waiting upon the Lord means what it says. The enemy wants to distract us from this because it is where we receive our inward strength. I've experienced the distractions, and I've found I not only have to evaluate priorities in my life, but also I have to get somewhere away from my phone, people, TV, or any other thing vying for my attention, to wait upon the Lord.

Take your Bible, a pen and paper, and read, meditate, and pray. God's Word promises us that when we have taken time to wait upon Him, we will not be shaken.

> *He gives strength to those who grow tired and increases the strength of those who are weak.*
> *Even young people grow tired and become weary, and young men will stumble and fall.*
> *Yet, the strength of those who wait with hope in the LORD will be renewed. They will soar on wings like eagles. They will run and won't become weary. They will walk and won't grow tired.*
> —ISAIAH 40:29–31, GW

Right after we surrendered our lives to the Lord in 1970, Billy Joe and I were told that we needed to make sure we had private time alone with God—individually. Sometimes people never realize the importance of this, and they become so accustomed to being with other people all the time that they don't know how to "be still, and know that I am God" (Psalm 46:10, NKJV).

Acts 4:13 (NIV) is an interesting verse: "When they [the religious leaders] saw the courage of Peter and John and realized that they were unschooled, ordinary men, they were astonished and they took note that these men had been with Jesus."

The time we spend alone with Jesus will be evident to others. Time with Jesus produces courage. Time with Him creates a willingness and a boldness to speak whatever He says. The more you spend time with Him, the more you will stop looking at your inadequacies, your failures, or what other people may think, and you will believe He is in you and for you to fulfill His purposes.

In my own life, I've realized 2 Corinthians 3:5–6 (NASB):

> *Not that we are adequate in ourselves to consider anything as coming from ourselves, but our adequacy is from God, who also made us adequate as servants of a new covenant, not of the letter but of the Spirit; for the letter kills, but the Spirit gives life.*

I've also experienced freedom within that my identity is not in a position, but it is in Jesus. This made it much easier to transition leadership to my son when the time came for him to become Lead Pastor.

I've found that my time alone with the Lord enabled me in how I related to people as a whole and helped me to follow His leading.

Your Key to Victory!

Trust is when we totally lean upon Jesus and the strength of His Word in our lives. As Proverbs 3:5 says, trusting in Him is not leaning to our own understanding or other people's understanding as far as that goes. It is continuing to acknowledge Him, believe, and walk with God no matter what we see or don't see regarding circumstances around us in this world.

Trust is believing that God will reveal what we need to know in time. It is taking each day at a time, following His guidance when we can't see ahead. It is knowing He has good plans for you and me, and that we have a future ahead of our lives. (See Jeremiah 29:11.)

Satan hates it when believers learn to enter into this secret place of trust in God because in doing that, they reject his lies.

Trust is our key to victory in every single day of this life.

Chapter 6

GRIEF

He was despised and rejected of men, a man of sorrows and acquainted with grief. And we hid, as it were, our faces from him...Surely he has borne our grief and carried our sorrows...he was wounded for our transgressions, he was bruised for our iniquities; the chastisement of our peace was upon him, and by his stripes we are healed...he was brought as a lamb to the slaughter, and as a sheep before its shearers is silent, so he opened not his mouth.

—Isaiah 53:3–5, 7, MEV

The writer, Isaiah, foresaw hundreds of years before Jesus Christ came to earth that He (the Messiah) would come to suffer and die as a sacrificial Lamb for all people. Isaiah saw the total redemption that Jesus would pay through His death, burial, and resurrection.

Jesus suffered on the cross for us in every way. He took our sin, our sufferings, pains, sorrows, and grief on the cross. Jesus identified with everything that affects us here in the earth and, in exchange, He gave us forgiveness, healing, freedom, comfort, and peace. Knowing this, whenever we experience the death of a loved one, we have this promise that as we draw close to Jesus, He has already experienced the sorrow and grief we feel, and He has removed the sting of death.

I remember when I was a kid, my brother showed me how to remove the stinger from a bee. Then he said, "It can't hurt you now."

First Corinthians 15:54–57 (NKJV) states:

> *So when this corruptible has put on incorruption, and this mortal has put on immortality, then shall be brought to pass the saying that is written: "Death is swallowed up in victory."*
> *"O Death, where is your sting?*
> *O Hades, where is your victory?"*
> *The sting of death is sin, and the strength of sin is the law. But thanks be to God, who gives us the victory through our Lord Jesus Christ.*

I realize this scripture is referring to the fact that we do not have to be afraid of death, because Jesus conquered the power of sin and death and has given us victory through Him. I also believe Jesus took the "stinger" out of death enveloping family members when a loved one dies. He has provided victory for those of us who are still here on earth. He enables us to overcome through His grace.

The Lord understands our humanity as well. He made us, and He put emotions within us. It is normal to shed some tears when your loved one has died, knowing you will not have their companionship or see them for a while. You know you will miss them. However, when your spirit dominates your life, you recognize that you are not helpless, so your emotions do not swallow you or overwhelm your life.

I believe there are different realms of emotion when someone dies at an earlier age than expected. It is more of a shock to the system of a person when a young child or a young spouse dies. When someone has lived a full life and they have had time to be prepared to step into eternity, there are tears of knowing they won't be with you on earth anymore, but a joy knowing they have finished their race and stepped into their rewards, and that one day you will see them again.

Emotions differ among people. Some people express their emotions more than others. People are raised in different environments and have varying personalities. Tears are a part of our emotional makeup and are not a sign of weakness. It's in knowing when we need to release our emotions and when we need to not let them control us.

Sometimes men tell a child, "Don't be a crybaby." I realize children need to be taught how to be tough and not weak or out of control. It is important to help children learn not to cry about everything that doesn't go their way. However, Ecclesiastes 3:4 (NLT) says it best that there is "a time to cry and a time to laugh. A time to grieve and a time to dance."

Since we live in an entitlement society where many parents, without realizing it, train their children to feel they are entitled to get everything they want, they cry when they don't get it. These children grow into adults who continue, many times, the habit of crying when they don't get what they want.

Life here on earth will not always be fair. Training children not to cry about everything is healthy. However, it is also healthy to teach them that there are times when it is okay to cry.

Dr. Judith Orloff wrote in *Psychology Today* magazine:

Tears are the body's release valve for stress, sadness, grief, anxiety, frustration, and joy. Tears are cleansing. Tears purge pent-up emotions so they can't lodge in the body as stress symptoms, such as fatigue or pain. Tears are beneficial to one's health and are not the sign of weakness but instead can be a sign of courage, strength, and authority. They are an expression of empathy which is the foundation of a morality and culture that is exclusively human.[7]

I believe there are times when tears are an expression of sensitivity and tenderness related to love, gratitude, and compassion.

Dr. Orloff also states:

Our bodies produce three kinds of tears:

1.   Reflex tears—enabling the eyes to clear noxious particles when irritated by smoke or exhaust;

2.   Continuous tears—keeps our eyes lubricated and protected from bacteria and infection, and these tears travel to the nose to keep the nose moist and bacteria-free; and

3.   Emotional tears—containing stress hormones which get excreted from the body from crying; these tears stimulate endorphins which is our body's natural painkiller and cause "feel good" hormones; these tears purify stress and negativity; in addition to physically detoxification, emotional tears heal the heart.[8]

---

7 Dr. Judith Orloff, *Psychology Today,* June 27, 2010, accessed online.
8 Ibid.

The day my husband died, my tears flowed along with the tears of family and friends. However, I did not feel hopeless, fearful, or resentful toward God. The years of my personal relationship with the Lord, the scriptures that my husband and I had memorized and spoken over our lives, and my husband's teachings flooded my mind and heart. I felt an undergirding in my life. It was as if I was surrounded in a cocoon of God's grace. I knew where Billy Joe was and that he was healed and happy.

I've thought about it and have concluded that whenever loved ones die and they go to heaven, they are not grieving. They are happy. It is we who are living on earth who have to overcome grief.

Billy Joe and I regularly had conversations about what really matters in life. The last few years of his life he had focused preaching on "living for eternity," "finishing strong," "reaching the harvest," "believers doing the work of the ministry," and "raising up the next generation."

After our family had cried the day of Billy Joe's promotion to heaven, we began to share stories about Billy Joe and what he meant to us. We shared tender memories of his impact upon our lives and funny memories that we all laughed about. In fact, by the third day I felt grief had lifted from me, and I was hearing God's thoughts and directions in my heart. Psalm 30:5 (NKJV) says, "Weeping may endure for a night, but joy comes in the morning."

I felt a strength that can only be attributed to God. Of course, there were times someone would stop to share a touching story of how Billy Joe had given them a word from the Lord that turned their life around, and it would bring a tear to my eyes. However, as soon as the tears came, they left.

Tears have come very easy for me throughout my life. I have had tears at times when I've ministered to individuals or heard a touching testimony or watched something on television that touched my heart because of self-sacrifice or seeing someone help someone in need.

I believe God can use tears to break down barriers of resentment and bitterness in other people's lives when you are in conversation with them. God is also drawn to tears of repentance and surrender to His will. All of these are healthy tears.

The Spirit of Grief (Unhealthy Tears)

Just as there are healthy tears, there are *unhealthy tears* also. There is a *spirit of grief* that tries to attach itself to someone who holds on to grief over a loved one. In reality, grief is not for the person who died. The person who is in heaven is not crying. They are happy. This means the tears we shed on earth are not for them. The tears we shed are for us, because we are thinking about ourselves not having them with us anymore.

The spirit of grief is self-focused, because it causes the person grieving to stay focused on what they don't have anymore, or what they may or may not have done, or what others should have or should not have done. Some people let the devil beat them up in their minds with condemnation. Others blame other people for all their troubles.

I've watched in some situations where a person continues crying or complaining or feeling hopeless (like giving up), and it began to take over the person's life. They couldn't seem to find anything to be thankful for. It is one thing to cry temporarily. It is another thing to allow grief to overpower your life. This is when grief becomes an oppressive spirit. It can affect not only the person grieving, but people in their life.

I remember encouraging a woman whose husband had died right before my husband passed away. Although she had two teenage daughters who were also grieving, she became engulfed with grief to the point that she stopped eating and plunged into depression. I was able to remind her that her daughters needed her more than ever during this time.

Because of other family members and friends from church, she began to gradually come out of that place of despair. She also faced a situation where other family members, beyond her immediate family, needed her help. She rose to not only be the mom for her daughters, but she temporarily took on other children to help in an urgent situation. Her focus was altered completely, and the depression faded away.

Two Women—Two Responses

The Bible gives us various examples of how people reacted when faced with tragedy or disappointment. One such story in the book of Ruth, is about two women and how they responded in two different ways regarding their husband's passing.

Naomi and her husband and two sons had moved to Moab. One son's name was Mahlon (meaning sick), and the other son's name was Chilion (meaning pining). It's interesting how these names foretold their future. The sons married Moabite women, Orpah and Ruth.

Naomi's husband died and over the next ten years the two sons died. Naomi was overwhelmed with grief and said that "the hand of the LORD is gone out against me" (Ruth 1:13). (Note: Too often people blame God for tragedy that comes their way. They don't realize or they forget that we live in a fallen world and we have an enemy, Satan, who seeks to steal, kill, and destroy.)

Naomi told her two daughters-in-law to return to their families, and she was going to move back to Bethlehem where she had come from. Orpah returned to her people, but Ruth had embraced the God of Abraham, Isaac, and Jacob, and she had rejected the gods of the Moabites. Ruth took on an attitude of faith and servanthood.

Ruth told Naomi, "I want to go with you. Your God shall be my God, and your people shall be my people." (See Ruth 1:16).

In those days people didn't usually leave their own race of people because it would be difficult to survive. It was a step of faith for Ruth to stay with Naomi. She could have been rejected by the Jewish community because of being a Moabite, but God's favor was upon her. God is drawn to an attitude of faith and servanthood.

Naomi's attitude was opposite of Ruth's. Naomi was bitter. (See Ruth 1:20-21.) She blamed God for her troubles. The spirit of grief causes a person to feel that God let them down. It can lead someone into depression. Naomi was struggling with depression and bitterness, but Ruth's attitude had a positive effect upon Naomi.

Naomi saw God's favor upon Ruth as she went to work in the fields. Because of Ruth's attitude, God moved in a way to restore Naomi's life and hers as well. He blessed them beyond what they could have imagined.

The story ended up with Ruth marrying Boaz, who owned the fields where she worked gathering grain. (Notice, Ruth went to work.

When people stay home and do nothing, depression sets in easier.) God honored Ruth for her faith and servant heart. He supplied all that she and Naomi needed, but also drew Ruth and Boaz together to fulfill His generational plan. Ruth was later listed in the genealogy of Jesus.

Getting Unstuck from Fear

Another way the devil tries to hinder people from going forward in life after a loved one passes is through the spirit of fear—fear of change, fear of disappointment or inadequacy, fear of lack, and fear of the future and the unknown. The spirit of fear can paralyze a person so they cannot rise up and move forward in life. They see life around them as hopeless.

Sometimes people feel they owe it to their loved one to stay in grief and not move forward. They think if they let go of the grief that it somehow dishonors their loved one.

One woman whose husband had been dead fifteen years would not touch or change his office fearing if she touched or sold his books it would be a sign of dishonor and disrespect. There comes a time when you must change things and even give some things away, realizing your loved one no longer needs those things, because in heaven they have everything and even more than they could ever want. Things on earth are temporary and corruptible, but things in heaven are glorious and incorruptible.

> For we know that when this earthly tent we live in is taken down (that is, when we die and leave this earthly body), we will have a house in heaven, an eternal body made for us by

God himself and not by human hands. We grow weary in our present bodies, and we long to put on our heavenly bodies like new clothing. For we will put on heavenly bodies; we will not be spirits without bodies. While we live in these earthly bodies, we groan and sigh, but it's not that we want to die and get rid of these bodies that clothe us. Rather, we want to put on our new bodies so that these dying bodies will be swallowed up by life.

—2 CORINTHIANS 5:1–4, NLT

Our loved ones in heaven are looking down at us on earth, wanting us to finish our race strong and not get stuck in grief. One woman whose husband passed blamed herself for his death because she convinced him to go with her to a concert, and as they returned home they had a car accident and he died. For fourteen years she went to his grave every morning and grieved that she had convinced him to go to something he really didn't want to attend, and that night he died.

The spirit of grief deceives a person into thinking they could have stopped something from happening and that same spirit holds people captive for years in condemnation and guilt. God is a God of freedom—not condemnation. If you feel you failed in some way, simply tell the Lord, turn it over to Him and let it go. Receive His freedom by faith. He will set you free from lying imaginations once you have awakened to the enemy's tactics and choose the freedom from grief and sorrow that Jesus provided on the cross. Then begin to meditate the Scriptures, letting Him wash over your mind and emotions.

When a person becomes preoccupied with a loved one's death, they miss opportunities for God to use their lives. One of the ladies in our church, whose husband had died and had at one time been on staff with us, came to this realization. Ethel had known the Word of God, but had been overcome with various thoughts and emotions after her husband passed. She went to a support group called "Grief Share." It was in this group that she was able to hear the stories of overcoming when a loved one passes and share her own story. Ethel found the freedom she needed from grief.

Afterward the leader approached her and said she believed that Ethel should start her own support group for people who had been stuck in grief to receive freedom. At first Ethel felt she could not do it, but God spoke to her to take the step of faith. She found that God's anointing was upon her to liberate others. Giving out of her own need, brought healing to her own life.

Now, over fourteen years later, she continues to bring healing and freedom to many lives. Ethel shared that she knew her obedience brought the power of God to others' lives, and her own life became even stronger. It was an opportunity she would have missed had she given in to her feelings not to do it. It takes faith to move beyond your feelings and obey the Holy Spirit's promptings in your life.

My mother-in-law has been an inspiration to me through the years. Her husband died at age 57 as well. I remember the day my husband and I arrived at the house after his father had died. Billy Joe's mom had been emotionally distraught. My husband laid hands on her and prayed over her, speaking the Word of peace into her. The house was full of people, and she told them what was needed, and then went to rest in her bed because she had been up the night before.

She shared that after everyone left and she was alone in the house, each day she sat down to read the Bible and pray, she felt grace surrounding her. A particular scripture seemed to rise up from the page of the Bible: "I am not alone, because the Father is with me" (John 16:32). Later, a friend had this scripture framed for her, and she has had it on her wall as a reminder ever since. She would go to work each day, and when she came home, she shared how she never felt lonely or alone.

A verse that ministered to me is Jeremiah 29:11 (NLT) where God said, "'For I know the plans I have for you,' says the LORD. 'They are plans for good and not for disaster, to give you a future and a hope.'"

Right after my husband passed, I found a handwritten note in his desk drawer which said, *"The joys of your future will swallow up the sorrows of your past."* I remembered when he preached this message many years before. I have kept that little note as a reminder to keep my focus on Jesus.

God also gave me the scripture in Philippians 1:21 (NASB): "For to me, to live is Christ and to die is gain." When you know you have a purpose for living here on earth that the Lord needs you to fulfill and you have eternity in your heart, knowing that heaven is ahead of you, there is a joy in living life.

The Holy Spirit Is Our Comforter

I believe the Holy Spirit cushions us emotionally, surrounding us with a cocoon of God's grace and divine empowerment. Second Corinthians 12:9–10 tells us when we feel weak within ourselves, He is strong and His grace is sufficient (more than enough) to strengthen us and empower us.

God brings comfort to us through the Holy Spirit. Our God is "the source of all comfort. He comforts us in all our troubles so that we can comfort others…" (2 Corinthians 1:3–4, NLT). God gives comfort and help to those who draw to Him in prayer, worship, and reading the Scriptures. When we draw to His presence, He gives comfort, strength, and guidance. He brings help into our lives and connects us with others who strengthen us as well.

In John 14:16 Jesus said He would send the Comforter to abide with us forever. Then in John 14:26 He said the Comforter is the Holy Spirit. In the original Greek, the word "Comforter" is *paraclete,* which means one called alongside another for help or counsel; helper, advocate, and comforter.

When my husband passed away and I moved into the leadership role at church, I lacked knowledge in certain areas. My husband had been gifted with a natural understanding of business and leadership skills. Along with this, he had gained knowledge over the years from experience in growing our ministry. There were things I had to learn, and I am still learning. Sometimes I felt overwhelmed, but the Holy Spirit would encourage me. For the most part, I leaned upon the gifting and skills of staff members around me whom God called to help me.

The first year after his passing, my mind was fuzzy and so was my memory at times. I am thankful for my family members and staff around me who supported me through those years. (My personal assistant was especially such a help.) Many times I spoke to myself words of faith: "I have the mind of Christ" (1 Corinthians 2:16). "My memory is blessed." (See Proverbs 10:7.)

I remember praying and fasting in the beginning of the second year, asking God for direction and for His vision for that year. One day I heard the strong witness in my spirit regarding God's direction of expansion. When I shared with our Associate Pastor what I had heard from the Holy Spirit, he encouraged my faith and presented the plan for which we could release our faith. It was a big step for us ($4.5 million in eighteen months to two years' time). We stretched our faith and shared the vision with our congregation who believed with us, and we reached our goal.

God gave us the word *momentum,* and He worked supernaturally. Over the entire five years, together as a church, we built the first Victory Bible College housing unit; produced a second 360° Life TV Series; expanded the Tulsa Dream Center; expanded the Victory Bible College, building a Food Distribution Center; purchased a second "99" tent for evangelism; laid a new turf football field/track; purchased more mobile kids trucks and busses; and started the second Victory Bible College housing unit. All of this was a supernatural work of God's grace.

Often I am reminded of the scripture in 1 Corinthians 1:27 (MSG): "God deliberately chose men and women that the culture overlooks...." This is so everyone knows only God could accomplish what is done for His Kingdom purposes.

Whatever we feel we lack within ourselves when we hear and obey God, He can work in a supernatural way. When we pray and give what we have, somehow the Holy Spirit moves among people and together we see great things.

John 14:26 says that the Holy Spirit wants to teach us and remind us of things we need to know. He has been my Advocate through testing times as well as my Counselor. In spite of my humanness when I've missed His direction at times, He has helped us, and He has delivered us. He has continued to reveal His thoughts and His ways to us as we seek Him. I am grateful He speaks into my life daily. I believe He will show His power in greater ways in the days ahead.

We Need Others

Church family and friends are important. Again I will say that I have been grateful for the people God has brought around my life to give me the support that I needed after Billy Joe passed. When I stepped into the role as Lead Pastor of our church, there were so many times that various staff members had the wisdom of God and the revelation of the Holy Spirit that we needed in moving forward with God's vision.

Realizing my need for a spiritual covering of other ministers in my life, the Holy Spirit directed me to ask certain ministers who believed in me and loved my husband to help me in this way. Various guest speakers, who were friends in ministry, came to speak to our congregation during the first year after Billy Joe passed. I waited for God to confirm who I was to ask, and He did. Pastor John Hagee was one who had spoken to me as he was leaving. He said, "If anyone gives you any trouble, pick up the phone and call me. I'll be there in a heartbeat." Not long after this, Bishop Keith Butler came to speak and afterward said about the same thing: "If anyone gives you trouble, just pick up the phone and call me." I was amazed how neither of these men had heard the other speak, and both had said the same thing.

I asked these two men and then some others to be a spiritual covering for me. Billy Joe and I would always say that we were low maintenance people. I don't call people for every little thing. I believe we need to be strong on our own and be able to hear from God, but we need to have people who we know are in our corner to counsel and pray with us when necessary.

When these men made these statements, it reminded me of when Billy Joe had left the college that we were both attending in Arkansas (SAU) to go to Oral Roberts University in Tulsa, Oklahoma. Billy Joe had been on the football team at SAU. He had witnessed to a lot of the guys on the team, and even though some didn't like anything religious, they respected him. They also seemed to feel responsible for me after Billy Joe left, because I was still at that college finishing my first year there. Billy Joe had transferred the middle of his sophomore year to ORU.

I mainly hung out with my older brother, David. David was not the size of these football players, and they seemed to feel responsible to protect both of us. There was a guy on campus who had been upset at David, and he had been flirting with me. One day three of the biggest football players came up to David and me and said, "Sharon, David, since Billy Joe isn't here anymore, we want you to know that if anybody, especially that one guy, gives you any trouble, we will take care of him or whoever it is." They were serious.

I am so grateful that God has always been there for me and that He has used many people around my life to stand with me. Even around our city, my husband had been a bridge builder with other pastors, so as I stepped forward in the Lead Pastor role, these pastors accepted me and encouraged me.

Now that my son Paul has stepped forward as Lead Pastor, I continue to serve in a support pastoral role to him and his wife, Ashley. My other son John and his wife, Charica, serve together with them as well. I also lead in various city, state, national, and international roles that I've been involved in through the years. I travel more, connecting and ministering beyond our home base.

My other children are ministering now in other states. My oldest, Sarah, and her husband, Caleb, and their children have a church—Victory Orlando—in Orlando, Florida. My daughter Ruthie and her husband, Adam, and their children travel in ministry to our Victory Leadership Network (VLP) of churches, based out of Texas.

Our lives are defined by our relationships. First, our relationship with God. Then our relationship with others—family, friends, church family, and others He connects us with. Relationships in life are extremely important. Many times we sow seeds in touching people's lives that God watches over. He causes those seeds to grow, and later we experience the fruit of those seeds. I am convinced that we continually sow all kinds of seeds throughout our lives that we reap in due season.

All the seeds of love and time that you sow to others will one day come back to you in your time of need. It may not come through the ones you sowed into, but God has a way of bringing the loving support you need when you need it most through members of the family of God.

Prophetic Word Through Pastor Ralph Wilkerson

God has sent various people into my life in various seasons who have given timely words of prophecy. One such word in due season came on October 20, 2011. Pastor Ralph Wilkerson, a friend in ministry happened to see me and gave me the following prophetic word of encouragement:

> There is a magnetic pull between heaven and earth.
> Billy Joe fulfilled his purpose and God's plan on earth.
> God's hand is upon you in a great way. He has greater things ahead that you will walk into.
> He is raising up women as yourself spiritually in this hour, and you can do it!
> Billy Joe still loves you dearly, and he's praying for you. Of course, Jesus is praying for you.
> There's an anointing with and in you that is going to be released in greater supernatural gifts of the Holy Spirit. It has to happen in these last days through those who will avail themselves to Him.

When this word was given to me, I knew the Lord was encouraging me not to focus on my inadequacies, but to see His hand upon my life and His supernatural empowerment to obey His calling.

Heaven has a word of encouragement to each of us when we look to the Lord.

Chapter 7

PROCESSING IT ALL AS A FAMILY

Billy Joe and I felt it was important to have family devotions with our children as they were growing up. We had this time each night. Anytime he and I were away, their grandmother prayed with them. These times were not spectacular, but they were consistent, which kept our relationship with our children real and genuine.

In these devotion times, we would read a Bible story or share from a Christian book, such as *Little Pilgrim's Progress*. Or sometimes Billy Joe would share the topic of what he was going to preach on the upcoming weekend at church. Then we would ask for their input. We had some interesting perspectives on these conversations, and some were funny.

At times when the kids were younger, they would act out the Bible story we shared with them. It was fun to watch each sibling direct another sibling and then not do exactly as they were told.

Each night we went around the circle of our family and prayed.

One night I remember our daughter Ruthie, who was about ten years old, prayed, "Lord, thank You that we shall live and not die to declare the works of the Lord." (This is from Psalm 118:17.) I thought it was interesting that she prayed that, because we had not been talking about that at all.

Later that same night, at 2:00 in the morning, our house had caught on fire. We were awakened suddenly in the quietness of that time, and we all escaped before fire burst out of all of the windows, licking the ground and fire that was 15 feet or higher engulfing our house as it came out of the roof.

Firemen came in four or five trucks, thinking they would be pulling out dead bodies. Instead, we were all alive. Ruthie's prayer was right on target.

Three weeks later we started going to Russia monthly for eighteen months to share the gospel. We knew the enemy tried unsuccessfully to keep us from going.

We encouraged our children that they had to have their own personal relationship with God. We knew we couldn't force this, but we knew we could prepare the way for them to see our lives and to hear our own stories of when we came to that point of surrender to heaven's calling on our lives.

I believe every person comes to that point of knowing and making the commitment to surrender to the calling of God. Each of them came to that place in their own lives, and then began reading the Bible on their own, establishing their time with God daily.

Today they refer back to some of the memories of our family devotions. They have also reflected upon seeing their dad in his time with the Lord and the impact it had upon them personally.

The father of a family has such a spiritual impact upon the spiritual destinies of his children, and many have underestimated this effect upon our society. Many children who have grown to become adults have behavioral problems because their fathers were not the spiritual leaders they needed to be.

When you have a strong foundation that has been laid in the home life, it affects how you view life, how you relate to others around you, how you respond to life experiences, and choices that you make as an adult later on. It's not just reading the Bible and praying that's important; it's about walking it out and genuinely allowing your children to see you walk it out.

After my husband died, our children had to process it with all they had been taught from my husband's teachings and his life. I knew what my husband and I had chosen to believe and stand fast upon. They had to grow through that time and rise to their belief in God and His Word being final authority in their own lives.

Each of our children—Sarah, Ruthie, John, and Paul—will share in the following pages how they handled the unexpected homegoing of their father and processed their thoughts and emotions.

Sarah Daugherty Wehrli

"Choosing to Live Awake to God's Purpose After My Father's Passing"

When my father, Pastor Billy Joe Daugherty, passed away in November 2009, it was one of the hardest things I have ever dealt with. He and my mom founded Victory Christian Center over thirty years ago, and I expected them both to be there for years to come.

My husband, Caleb, and I were living on the mission field in Asia when we got news of my dad's declining health. Family informed us that we needed to come home immediately, so we hurried back to Tulsa. Within a few hours of arriving, my dad went to be with Jesus at only 57 years old.

It was not easy. I was close to my dad and looked up to him in so many ways. But more importantly, he was my hero. After his passing, I had a lot of questions like, *Why did this happen, and what am I supposed to do now?* In the natural, it would have been easy for me to curl up in depression and confusion, but God reminded me that He still had a plan for my life and that there were assignments He had called me to fulfill on this earth.

Five days after my dad's funeral, Caleb and I were scheduled to fly back to Cambodia. We were hosting a Christmas gift giveaway outreach for hundreds of children in remote villages, as well as hosting a women's conference and finishing a church building project we had started there.

At that time, I didn't feel like going or that I had much hope to offer them, so I debated on whether to go with Caleb or just stay home.

But when I went to my mom to ask what she thought I should do, she reminded me of Jesus' example in Mark 6 when He heard that His cousin, John the Baptist, had been beheaded. It says that Jesus was grieved at the news and went to find a solitary place across the water. But when He got to the other side, there were multitudes of people waiting to hear from Him. Matthew 9:36 (NKJV) says, "When He [Jesus] saw the multitudes, He was moved with compassion for them, because they were…like sheep having no shepherd." So He began to teach them.

After Jesus taught, the people were hungry. Jesus told His disciples to get them something to eat. But all they could find was a little boy with a small lunch of five loaves and two fish. He offered what he had to Jesus, and Jesus blessed it. That day this little boy's lunch was supernaturally multiplied to feed over 5,000 men, plus women and children!

After sharing that story with me, my mom said, "Sarah, I believe if you will go in the midst of your own pain and loss, offer what is in your hand, and just love the precious people of Cambodia, Jesus will do miracles."

I knew in my heart that my mom was right, and when I prayed, God reminded me of a dream I had just had a few months before. In the dream, I was standing in a circle of people, and it seemed as though we were all waiting for something. It didn't take me long to realize we were waiting for orders. We had a mission to complete, and each of us was given individual assignments to fulfill. As I glanced to my right, I noticed the girl next to me was curled up in a fetal position asleep, and I thought, *Why is she sleeping? She needs to wake up! We have a job to do!*

When I got up, I sensed God was trying to speak to me. So I asked Him what the meaning of this dream was. He said the circle of people represented the body of Christ, and each person has a part to play and a divine assignment to fulfill (as 1 Corinthians 12 expounds more upon). But some have chosen to fall asleep instead of walking in their calling because of tragedy, hurt, or fear.

The Lord reminded me of that word and said, "Sarah, you can curl up in hurt and depression, or you can wake up and rise up and pursue the divine assignment I have for you."

I went on that trip to Cambodia five days after the funeral. As I was there, something supernatural happened. A joy came into my heart that was unexplainable. Not only that, but people were saved and healed by the power of God as we went.

Through many dear friends and partners, God supernaturally provided for the Christmas gift bags to be distributed to hundreds of children, along with food for families; and fresh water wells were dug in several of the villages. It was beautiful to see hundreds of women ministered to through the women's conference and to see the walls of the church building being put up. We saw God multiply our loaves and fishes, and it was miraculous!

While I was there, God did something else in my heart that will mark me forever. One night I walked into one of the churches and saw about thirty orphans sleeping on the floor. I asked the pastor about the kids and what we could do for them. He said, "These children are orphans, and because they have nowhere else to go, we let them sleep on the floor of the church at night." I knew in my heart that we needed to do something, but I didn't know how.

I wrote out the vision to build a children's home, and then began to share it with the church we were a part of in Hong Kong. In ten days God miraculously provided all the funds to build the first Hope for Children home. The local pastors agreed to run the home and are passionate about raising those children to know Christ and follow His plan for their lives. This started a chain reaction of other homes being built in surrounding nations. Since that time, God has helped us connect others with this vision, and today many homes have been raised up there and in other nations.

As I reflect back to that season of my dad's passing, I think about how sometimes we can only see the pain right in front of us and want to give up on the purpose God has for us. But if we will press through and fix our eyes on Jesus, He will give us strength to wake up and rise up. He reminds us that there are always people on the other side of our obedience. He can bring beauty from ashes and joy where there has been sorrow. For me, after my dad passed I was awakened even more so to make the most of the opportunities God has put before me and to realize that I have a unique purpose to walk out.

Ephesians 5:11, 14–17 (MSG) says:

> Don't waste your time on useless work, mere busywork, the barren pursuits of darkness…Wake up from your sleep…Christ will show you the light! So watch your step. Use your head. Make the most of every chance you get. These are desperate times! Don't live carelessly, unthinkingly. Make sure you understand what the Master wants.

My husband, Caleb, and I stayed overseas for another seven months to fulfill commitments we had there, and then felt God calling us back to Tulsa to be a support to my mom in the church. We didn't know how long that season would be, but we knew it was what we were supposed to do in that time.

Going back home to the USA was more of a culture shock for me than it was when I first moved overseas, but I knew God had a purpose for bringing us back. It was a challenging season to navigate for us and also for the church, but I'm grateful that God's grace and anointing were on my mom to be the lead pastor during that time.

I am also thankful for all the amazing people who are a part of the church family who stayed with us during this time. The church wasn't built on a man, but on the solid rock of Jesus. Even when things are shaken, if our faith is in Jesus, then we will be able to stand.

Something my parents taught me that helped me during this time was to not base my faith on the experiences of man but on the authority of God's Word. Ultimately, my relationship with Jesus, knowing He was for me and He was with me, helped me through those challenging times. It was in times of worship, tears, and prayer that He reminded me of His love and purpose for my life. He also began to expand my vision for things ahead. It was during this time that the Lord began to put in our hearts the desire to plant a church.

In 2014 we stepped out in faith to plant a life-giving church, and it has been amazing to see all God has done through that step of faith. We are overwhelmed with gratitude and full of vision for what He will continue to do through Victory Orlando.

As we begin to wake up to God's purpose for our lives, we will quickly find that it's "others-centered." In other words, it revolves around people. My encouragement to you is no matter what you have gone through, draw near to Jesus, let Him awaken your heart to His purpose and the people He has called you to reach. Then, boldly rise up in faith and begin stepping out in what He says. You are here on this planet for such a time as this. Live on purpose and make the most of every opportunity!

It's time to wake up...

Out of fear and into faith.
Out of discouragement and into hope.
Out of guilt and into freedom.
Out of worry and into peace.
Out of selfishness and into love.
Out of bitterness and into forgiveness.
Out of comparison and into knowing your identity in Christ.
Out of weariness and into God's strength.
Out of distraction and into purpose.

Ruthie Daugherty Sanders

Back in December 2009 and January 2010...

When my dad passed away, my first thoughts and emotions were sadness. I was going to miss him so much. He was my dad. I knew he was in heaven, and his body was healed. It was still tough to realize he was gone from this earth, and I wouldn't see him anymore. He would not be there when I had my children or get to be a part of their lives. I reflected on the days leading up to his death, how he was so sick; we prayed and believed in God, and did all we could do to get him the best medical help possible. So many thoughts and emotions flooded me.

God reminded me of something that He spoke to me just a few hours earlier that night, that if he were to pass that it would only catapult each of us kids into the ministry and callings that God had for us. It would not diminish us or hold us back, but it would increase us in all that God had placed on the inside of us. As long as Dad was around, we each led under him, but now that he had passed, it was time for us to step up and step out boldly.

As weeks passed, I began to have an identity crisis. My family, my church, and my work had all been changed dramatically. I was missing a major person in all of those areas. In so many ways, my life was wrapped around serving my father in ministry work, in the church as my pastor, and in our family as my father. My husband and I were heavily involved in the work of the church.

Earlier that year of 2009, I had taken a job that my dad had presented to me. He was updating the television ministry, which affected the entire TV and media department and the prayer line. So I took on the responsibility of overseeing those departments and that process under his direction. On top of these areas, I took on the administrative oversight of the children's and nursery departments. I was stretched beyond what I ever thought I could do. It was during that season that my dad pushed me even more, and I learned so much about leading and making decisions on a large scale for a mega church. I sought to predict his decisions before he made them so he wouldn't have to, in order for him to trust me to lead. I became closer to my dad in those nine months.

When my dad got sick, I sat at the hospital many days and nights with him and my mom. I would bring my computer to type what he needed or to show him things that he wanted to see that related to the church. Once he was gone, I didn't know what to do. I immediately began to help my mom because I knew she didn't know all the details of everything, but I still wasn't sure if that was the right thing to do. I questioned why I existed. I wondered what my life was going to be about now that he was gone. In my mind, I thought, "God had called me to serve my dad so now what am I supposed to do? Is my life over? Should I just stop living?"

The Holy Spirit began to remind me of my heavenly Father and that my life is about the calling He has for me. The Lord led a person across my path who was serving on staff at Victory who had walked through a similar situation with losing her father. She shared her story with me. She told me that she went through an identity crisis as well, but she overcame it by really knowing God as her heavenly Father. It was something she had always known, but He became more real to her as a Father after her dad passed.

I realized I had put so much trust and reliance on my earthly father that I had not shifted my focus and my dependence onto my heavenly Father. Once I was able to do that, all the fear and worry about who I was and my future lifted off me. I realized my life was established on Jesus and His Word, and that I would continue to follow God's call on my life. Just because my dad was no longer here on earth didn't mean that my calling had ended. I was just in a new season. I accepted that revelation of God as my Father and began to rely on Him in an even greater way.

My life became about serving the Kingdom of God, not a man or a woman. It's about pleasing and obeying God. So much joy was brought back into my life when I got that revelation. I found a new freedom in Christ, because my identity was not in my work or whom I worked for, it was in Christ!

John Daugherty

The only difference between you and that person you really admire is their perspective. You can change your life and others by changing your perspective. I saw this with my dad growing up. There would be times when nothing was going right in ministry, finances, and even relationships, yet he would stay positive. He would never talk about people behind their back, even when I knew someone had done him wrong. His outlook was, no bad happening can steal your joy; you can only give it away. I admired his perspective, because he helped me utilize it through life's trials.

"When people give you hell, give them heaven. Bring heaven down to earth." These were words my dad said to me at a point in my life when I was deeply hurt. I had no idea how powerful those words were until I realized I was going to use those words the rest of my life.

When my dad passed, someone came up to me and told me my dad's death was a judgment. Those words were pretty harsh. Sometime later, my wife and I went through a difficult test that God delivered our lives through, and the pain it brought to both of us was really heavy. I remembered those words my dad lived by: "When people give you hell, give them heaven."

If you live in the world, bad things happen to good people. I have found that the more impact you want to make in the world, the more the attacks will come. Galatians 6:9 tells us to not grow weary in well doing, for in due time we will reap a harvest.

My healing would come through planting seeds of heaven in people's lives. My life goal after Dad passed became to reach as many people for Jesus as possible. I wanted to honor my dad. I loved him, but I believe I valued him even more after he had passed.

From a young age, I grew up respecting my dad and loving him, but I didn't value his parenting all the time. My siblings all grew up singing in worship and being involved in ministry through their own choice. I did not want to do ministry. There were times when I did funny sketches for youth and the college ministry, but most of them were deemed too edgy or inappropriate.

My dad would get e-mails about my conduct and behavior in high school and college, and because he loved me, I was disciplined a lot. Even getting spanked after my eighteenth birthday! Ha! So naturally as a "grown man," I resented my dad, thinking he was too strict.

I tried avoiding him as much as I could in college, even at times blocking his cell number! Then those situations would happen when my stupidity would leave me alone with no one else to talk to, so I would call my dad. He was the only person I trusted, because I trusted his character. I think he grew in his discipline of me, of guiding me and not condemning me.

The last year of my dad's life, we got really close. I'm so thankful I had that last year, because it helped with my healing.

The last year of my dad's life, I realized how much he was pouring into me. He would ask me, "Who are you raising up?" I was serving in our Junior High ministry at the time. I was doing it just because it was fun. But after my dad said that, I began to realize these young boys in the Junior High ministry were looking for someone to disciple them and call out the man of God in them.

I became intentional about daily and weekly checking up on these sixth, seventh, and eighth grade boys. We would do river raft trips, paintball wars, hiking, etc. As I began doing this, I felt like I was planting seeds into the future of Victory Church.

I became excited and drove to my parents' home to tell my dad what I was doing with these young men. He would say, "Wow, John! Now that is leaving a legacy! Train them up to train others up." As he validated my efforts, I began to really value and enjoy ministry and to recognize God's calling on my life.

After my dad passed, I was given the responsibility of being over the whole youth ministry, sixth through twelfth grade! At first I was intimidated, because my college education was in sports training. Our Assistant Pastor, Bruce Edwards, helped me so much during that time. He said, "John, ministry is like coaching. You are training up the leaders of tomorrow. Your dad did it, and you can do it too."

I began to take a whole different approach in ministry. I fell in love with it, and I also fell in love with a girl my dad had been rooting for the last eight years of my life.

Six months after my dad passed, I married Charica Jacobs. For many years, her family worked at our Tulsa Dream Center with our outreach youth. My dad told me to take her to a football banquet my freshman year, because he loved her spirit and her heart after God. After that banquet and until we started dating, he would always bring her up and ask, "How's Charica? She's a powerhouse, and I think you need someone to tame you." I brushed it off for a few years until I finally grew up and realized he was right!

On our wedding day we did worship songs that were my dad's favorites in order to honor him. And I knew he was throwing a party in heaven watching me marry the girl he knew from the beginning was "the one."

My wife and I loved serving at the church. We would meet people outside of the four walls who would talk about what my dad did for them. During that time, I was working out at a YMCA where there was a special needs guy who was faithfully there every time I walked in. He would be racking weights or cleaning off equipment with a rag. Everyone knew him. He was so nice and talkative to everybody.

One day he came up to me and said, "Hey, John! I knew your dad. Well, I watched him on TV. I got a small book he wrote just for me. It's purple, and it says 'You have a purpose.' I miss him, but I know I have a purpose here. Anyway, that's all..." and he walked off hurriedly.

I couldn't help but tear up right there in the gym. Not just because of the impact my dad made on this young man at the YMCA, but that he trained up a leader and those words that young man said, "I miss him, but I know I have a purpose here." It kept me grounded that my purpose here on earth is much greater than any pain I felt from my dad's loss. I knew I should never stop doing my purpose.

My dad and I would dream of creative ways to reach people for Jesus. I would tell him what was boring about church, or our average illustrated sermon productions, and he would listen. That was my favorite thing to know he was listening. It showed that he cared. A word to fathers: If you want your children to feel valued, be intentional in listening to them.

I wasn't perfect, and my dad explained how he wasn't perfect either. My dad could have fooled me! I thought he had never sinned. His openness with me, as I got older, made me value his parenting even more. He figured out my passion for ministry may not have been preaching or worshiping, but it was through the creative arts. He fueled that fire.

Today, I'm honored to serve at Victory in various roles and one of those roles is in the Creative Department, working on reaching the world through creative arts. Every time I write a script, or we do a photo shoot, or a film that presents the gospel, I feel as if I'm doing it in honor of my dad.

Healing comes every time I get a new idea or accept a new challenge in finding ways to reach more people for Jesus because I miss my dad, but I know I have a purpose here!

As far as Dad's death, I grieved and felt a tremendous loss, but then I turned it into a mandate to do my part to complete the vision that God gave my father.

I was so determined to fulfill the vision that originated with my dad: Reaching as many people as possible for Jesus; growing Victory Christian School; growing Victory's impact on the world; and consistently bringing up young men specifically and raising them into leaders—those my dad always said were mighty men whom he spoke over in the school. I felt strongly that the mantle of calling out young men fell on me.

So how do I feel about my dad's death? It was a mandate to me and a charge—not a loss!

Paul Daugherty

I'll never forget coming to the hospital October 1st—the day that my father was admitted to St. John's Hospital in downtown Tulsa, Oklahoma. My mom called and said, "Paul, you need to come now to the hospital and join the rest of the family to pray over Dad."

I was confused. I had never seen my dad severely sick or ever in a hospital bed. When I got to the hospital room and saw him lying there on the bed and then heard from the doctor that he had a very aggressive type of cancer, I lost it emotionally. I began to cry and spiral down mentally trying to figure out why this was happening to my dad and to our family, just two weeks before I was to get married.

The doctors told us that he could fight it, but it would have to be confronted quickly with all kinds of treatment, including chemotherapy. I remember my dad telling me, "Paul, it's going to be okay. We trust in God no matter what."

I was getting married on October 16th, and my father was convinced that he would be the one to marry us on our wedding day. He had just finished a serious round of treatment and yet he asked if we would move our wedding to October 17th so he could come and perform our wedding. We, of course, changed the wedding date.

I remember waiting at the altar with my bride-to-be, Ashley, as he came in to our church that day. The crowd erupted in applause as he welcomed everyone and then performed our wedding.

We had a lot of talks throughout my lifetime, but the talks I had with him those last two months that he was alive were much different. It's like he knew his time was running out, and he would drop little hints to me about the church, about ministry, about family, and about living for God. He was making sure that we all knew how important we were to him and how important a personal relationship with God was.

The week before Thanksgiving he and I talked about how we were going to eat some good home-cooked food at Gran Gran's (his mom, my grandma). The following week is when he was life-flighted from Tulsa Cancer Treatment Center to MD Anderson Hospital in Houston. Our family was huddled around his bed, praying.

The night before he passed away, some of the family had walked out of his room briefly, and I was in the room with him all alone. His body was fading out and shutting down, and he couldn't open his eyes or his mouth, but I knew he was listening. I was crying over his bed and just praying that God would breathe resurrection life over him. As I was holding his cold hand, I felt a surge of electricity flowing out of his hand into mine. It was as if God was allowing him to release anointing, and it felt like there was a download of something powerful going into me.

As each sibling and my mom came back into the room, we kept praying, and I didn't leave his side. His heartbeat began to flatline, and we prayed for a long time for resurrection life.

After praying strong and asking others who had called on the phone, or contacted us from around the world, or came in person that night to pray, we felt something had changed in the spirit realm in that room. It was like each of us knew my dad was smiling from heaven, like a runner who had just finished his race and was finally finished. We all, as a family, sensed the presence of God in the room, and we began to worship and sing songs together as we cried and mourned the physical loss of our father, pastor, and friend.

Right after my father passed, while we were singing songs, I felt God's voice speaking to me. It was more real than a close friend talking to me. It was as if my dad and God and Jesus were all standing by each other in heaven looking down through the clouds at us. And God said, "Paul, serve your mom, serve the church, and get ready, because you will soon be the pastor of Victory."

When I heard God speak those words, I was filled with all kinds of emotions and questions and grief. I kept that word to myself for almost a year before telling my wife. I am the youngest of four, each having a ministry calling on their lives. Besides being the youngest, I knew I wasn't even close to being qualified to do what my dad did, but God began developing things in me over that time after my father passed that I never knew were inside me.

After that day, November 22, 2009, it took me at least eight months to really emotionally move on. I would often wake up in the middle of the night having nightmares of the church, my family, and my father. I would cry every day, and some days were worse than others. I remember just feeling depressed walking into the church for that whole eight months and oftentimes that following year. But I would be reminded of God's Word that my parents had spoken to us since we were young about choosing joy and not allowing a spirit of despair to rule our hearts.

I remember reading a few books that really helped me to break out of that depression and despair. One of the books that majorly impacted me was *Every Day a Friday: How to Be Happier 7 Days a*

Week by Joel Osteen. I wasn't a big reader, but I read that book almost three times. Each time I read it, I would cry and laugh and just start erupting into praise to God that He was giving me *joy* again.

I also had to regain my trust and faith that God could heal people after walking through that experience with my father. I had a hard time going back into hospitals and praying for people who were sick for the first nine months after my father had passed. But while I was on a mission trip in Brazil, God spoke to me to pray for people to get healed. In fact, God used a young Brazilian pastor to really challenge me that week while our church team was in San Paulo doing a crusade.

On the last night of the crusade, the pastor asked me to step up and do an altar call for people who needed healing. I told him that I was the wrong guy for the job and that I had gone through a tough experience of not seeing my prayers get answered for my dad to be healed.

Then this pastor told me, "Paul, the day before your team arrived here in Brazil, my thirty-three-year-old wife died of lymphoma cancer, and I was devastated. But she told me right before she died that she wanted me to keep praying for others to be healed and to never allow experience to change our theology that God is still a *healer.*"

Then he said, "I didn't want to join your team this week in ministry, because I was grieving. But when I heard about what you, Pastor Paul, walked through with your dad and that you came here to Brazil to preach and minister, I knew I needed to be with you guys this week and receive my emotional healing." He continued, "So Paul, I will be your translator if you are willing to let God use the two of us through our pain to let His healing power flow tonight."

After that, I couldn't resist. I stepped up with him that night with both of us in tears and began praying for people to be healed and watched as God opened blind eyes, dissolved tumors, and healed so many people of various diseases.

I know that my father was smiling ear to ear and still is today watching each of his kids walk out our destinies that God called us to walk in. And I also know that my father did not die in vain. His life was well lived and was a seed in the ground for so many who have now come into the Kingdom because of his sacrifices.

In August of 2014, I stepped into the role of Lead Pastor at our church at Victory, and I have felt God's hand on my life so strongly in all of my inadequacies and insufficiencies. I can hear my dad cheering from heaven, "Come on, Paul. You've got what it takes because God is with you, for you, and in you. Finish strong. Don't give up. Don't lose hope. Stick with it!"

I can say that today my heart is healed from the pain of losing my dad, and I still have my moments of tears but now those tears are filled with joy, knowing that I will see him again and that he's joined with the angels celebrating God's faithfulness in his life and the legacy he left behind!

Part 2

_____

KEYS TO
OVERCOMING

Chapter 8

GOD IS WITH YOU— LETTING HIS WORD SPEAK TO YOU

So do not fear, for I am with you; do not be dismayed, for I am your God. I will strengthen you and help you; I will uphold you with my righteous right hand.

—Isaiah 41:10, NIV

The greatest comfort you can know is that God is with you and that He will help you. I realize that because you cannot see God with your natural eyes that sometimes your mind may question, "How do I know God is with me?" It's called faith.

Jesus said, "Blessed are those who believe without seeing me" (John 20:29, NLT). Hebrews 11:6 (GNT) tells us, "Whoever comes to God must have faith that God exists and rewards those who seek him." Faith is based upon God's covenant promises, which are found in the Bible. I've never seen God physically, but I know God through His Word and by my relationship with Him through listening to His Holy Spirit's voice in my heart.

Through prayer I talk to Him, and He speaks His thoughts into my heart. When I ask Him for specific help regarding situations, I have seen His intervention. There are times when He has sent people to help and give insight, and then there are times when He has worked in situations supernaturally.

I was accustomed to having Billy Joe as a close companion in life, helping me and giving me input. Suddenly he was no longer with me anymore. I have become much more aware of my dependence upon God's help and His insight since Billy Joe's passing.

As I've ministered to others over the years, I have noticed that sometimes the enemy tries to make a person feel that God is far away and that He is not listening. God is present with you. In fact, Psalm 46:1 says, "God is our *refuge* and *strength*, a *very present help* in trouble" (emphasis mine).

Always go back to God's Word to hear what He says to you. Psalm 46:10 tells us to be still and know that He is God, and He will be exalted in our lives. The main concern regarding this verse is finding a place to be still and wait upon Him.

Sometimes we have to make ourselves sit still to read God's Word, memorize Scripture, and pray. When someone gets still and turns off all other distractions, God's Word will speak peace and counsel to your soul.

Isaiah 40:29–31 (NKJV) says: "He gives power to the weak (to overcome), and to those who have no might He increases strength. Even the youths shall faint and be weary, and the young men shall utterly fall, but those who wait on ["wait" in the Hebrew is *qavah,* which means to bind together like rope strands wrapping around each other to become a strong cord; it also means to come to God and expect something] the LORD shall renew their strength ["renew" in Hebrew is *chalaph,* which means to be changed, new, to go forward, to strike through the enemy, to rise up]; they shall mount up with wings like eagles [soar above the clouds; they rise above the storm. It's an interesting comparison that God makes with the eagle. An eagle will rise and press beyond the storm to a higher level where it is peaceful. Other birds stay low under the storm and seek to find shelter in bushes or trees, but they struggle going through the storm.]; they shall run and not be weary, they shall walk and not faint."

We all face times when we feel weak, but when we take time alone with God to pray and read the Word, God strengthens us. When we take time alone with God, seeking Him, reading His Word, waiting upon Him, He wraps Himself around us and changes us.

He changes our thoughts, and His peace calms our emotions. He gives us His thoughts, and He works on our behalf regarding our circumstances. Sure, it takes time, but later we will look back and see how He made a way many times when there seemed to be a roadblock. He helps us to strike through the enemy's lies and negative thoughts. He helps us rise up and go forward. Strength comes for us to continue on and not get weary, faint, or quit.

God's Enablement

Throughout Scripture, we see this phrase, "The Lord is with you." After Moses died and Joshua was responsible to lead God's people to possess the Promised Land, he knew there were giants, walled cities, and multitudes of enemies ahead. He also knew Moses had had the respect of the people because they had seen signs, wonders, and miracles God had performed throughout Moses' leadership.

Years before, Joshua and Caleb had been the only two spies who had boldly proclaimed, "We are well able to go up at once and possess the land," knowing that God was with them. However, now Joshua is the leader. He knew God was with him, but he also knew he had never done what Moses was able to do. He knew he needed God's confirming signs and wonders to lead the people.

God said to Joshua three times in Joshua chapter 1, "Be strong and courageous" (NKJV). In Joshua 1:5 (NKJV) He said, "As I was with Moses, so I will be with you...." Then God reaffirmed him and said, "Have I not commanded you? Be strong and of good courage; do not be afraid, nor be dismayed, for the LORD your God is with you wherever you go" (v. 9).

As I read this scripture, God spoke to me that even though someone we love, admire, and hold in high esteem passes away, God is still with us, and He will enable us to carry out His plan. I knew God was with me and that I had heard from Him, but I knew I was not my husband and that there were areas where I lacked knowledge.

It's easy to feel inadequate when we compare ourselves with others who have gone before us. This is why God told Joshua that *He would be with him as He was with Moses.* Did that mean that Joshua would carry a rod like Moses did and perform the same signs and wonders, or talk to a burning bush?

When God says He will be with us as He was with others, it doesn't mean we will become just like these people who lived before. What it does mean is that He is with us with His same power to enable us to do whatever He says. It will simply require us to take some steps of faith and obedience to His voice.

Think about it! Joshua didn't have a rod. It's interesting that the first miracle was to cross a huge river with women and children. When Joshua led them to step into the water with faith, the waters parted just as they did when Moses led them through the Red Sea. After this, it was steps of faith and obedience by Joshua and all the people that led them to possess the Promised Land.

Moses and Joshua were two different people and were gifted differently by God, but God used both of them. We can never replace those who have gone before us, but we can allow God to show Himself strong in our lives.

God Will Continue to Tell Us to Be Strong and Courageous

When the angel of the Lord appeared to Gideon in Judges 6:12 (NET), and said, "The LORD is with you, courageous warrior!" Gideon had been hiding in fear because of the oppression of the Midianites. Gideon's response was, "'Pardon me, but if the LORD is with us, why has such disaster overtaken us? Where are all his miraculous deeds our ancestors told us about?' They said, 'Did the LORD not bring us up from Egypt?' But now the LORD has abandoned us and handed us over to Midian" (v. 13, NET).

Gideon got into his reasoning here. When heaven sends a supernatural direction to you, it doesn't pay to argue and reject what is being said to you.

"Then the LORD himself turned to him and said, 'You have the strength. Deliver Israel from the power of the Midianites! Have I not sent you?' Gideon said to him, 'But LORD, how can I deliver Israel? Just look! My clan is the weakest in Manasseh, and I am the youngest in my family.' The LORD said, 'Ah, but I will be with you! You will strike down the whole Midianite army'" (vv. 14–16, NET).

When God says He will be with us, then whatever He tells us to do, we will not be doing it on our own. His supernatural help, ability, favor, and protection will be there with us.

After this Gideon still wasn't convinced, so he asked for a sign. God was merciful and gave him a sign, and God used Gideon to defeat the Midianites.

This story again shows how God wants us to know that He is with us and that He will work supernaturally in our behalf as we believe in Him and obey Him. God called Gideon "courageous," even when Gideon was anything but!

God believes in people and sees potential in each of our lives. He also calls things that be not as though they were (see Romans 4:17), because He is a God of faith. God believes you are courageous, especially if you have received Jesus into your heart.

Gideon may have questioned God to start, but God spoke strength into him to rise up and believe that He could use him to help deliver others.

God sees what He can do through us if we can believe and allow Him to work in our lives. He sees Himself with us and enables us to do what we could not do in our own natural ability.

God's Companionship

"I am not alone, because the Father is with me."
—JOHN 16:32

God is not only with you to do what you need to do, He is also with you to meet that deep emotional need of companionship. You do not have to feel lonely. Loneliness is an attitude causing a depressing feeling of being alone without friendly companionship or support. You can actually have this attitude and be among other people who are friendly and supportive. Loneliness is a spirit that tries to come upon people to depress them and make them vulnerable to further assaults of the enemy.

My mother-in-law, Iru Daugherty, experienced her husband passing away at the young age of 57. My husband and I were with her right after Mr. Daugherty passed away. We prayed with her, and then Billy Joe said, "Mom, you can sit in a rocker and just rehearse the past memories, or you can rise up, and God can use your life."

Both of us received and shared Isaiah 58 with her about the chosen fast, which instructs us to live a life that reaches out to others in need. When we reach out to others to help them, our light will rise in obscurity. Isaiah 58:8 (AMP) says:

> *"Then your light will break out like the dawn,*
>   *And your healing (restoration, new life) will quickly spring forth;*
>   *Your righteousness will go before you [leading you to peace and prosperity],*
>   *The glory of the LORD will be your rear guard.*

The *Dake's Bible* says that "your light will burst forth like the beams of the sun on a clear morning, your darkness be as the noonday."[9] God lifts the person who turns to help others; healing comes into their heart, and the power of a new life begins to rise within.

Iru worked each day and began to go to the nursing home regularly after work to visit people she did not know before. She became involved in an interdenominational women's ministry and developed new friendships. One friend gave her a small plaque one day that she still has today hanging on her wall, which quotes the scripture, "I am not alone, because the Father is with me" (John 16:32).

She shared with us later how she never felt alone, even though she was suddenly living alone. She was never lonely. She began each day with prayer and reading the Bible; then she went to work. God made His presence very real to her. Even when she moved from the town she had lived in for years and left these friends behind, moving to our city, she began to make new friends and still has friends today who are both young and old.

God wants to make His presence very real to you too. He doesn't want you to be lonely. He is with you, and He wants to speak to you each day. He also wants to use the body of Christ around your life to strengthen you, and He wants to use your life to help others. It's the principle of sowing and reaping. When you give, it comes back into your life. Your own emotional needs are restored and joy comes again.

After my husband passed away, I wanted to be with our church family to worship with them, to hug them, and to pray for others.

---

9 Finis Jennings Dake. *Dake's Annotated Reference Bible,* Dake's Bible Sales, Lawrenceville, GA, 1963, 1991, 724.

Avoid Isolation

It's important not to become isolated after a loved one passes away. Being with others strengthens us. First Corinthians 12:12–27 tells us that we are the body of Christ, and each part is important.

God designed the body of Christ like a physical body in such a way that the members must care for one another. If one member suffers, all the members suffer with him or her; or if one member is honored, then all the members rejoice with him or her. It's the love of Christ that connects us and flows through us, keeping His body healthy and strong.

Hebrews 10:25 says that as Jesus' return draws near, we need to encourage and help one another, not avoiding worshiping together but spurring each other on.

I find that people who walk in victory after a loved one passes away have certain habits in life that help them, and one of those habits is always staying connected with a local church body and reaching out to others in some way.

Scriptural Confessions to Activate Your Faith

I have found that as I've meditated on Scripture when I speak them they give me confidence and assurance.

Here are some scriptural confessions to activate your faith; and as you speak them, envision the Lord fulfilling these promises in your life:

Psalm 27:1—

The LORD is my light and my salvation, Whom shall I fear?

The LORD *is the strength of my life. Of whom shall I be afraid?*

Hebrews 13:5–6—

The Lord will never leave me or abandon me. He is my Helper. I will not be afraid (Author paraphrase).

Zephaniah 3:17—

The LORD *my God is in the midst of my life and He is mighty, a warrior bringing victory; He will create calm in my life with His love, and He will rejoice over me with singing* (Author paraphrase).

John 16:32—

I am not alone, because the Father is with me.

Psalm 46:1-2—

God is my refuge and my strength, a very present help in time of trouble. Therefore I will not be afraid (Author paraphrase).

Isaiah 41:10—

I will not fear, for God is with me. He will strengthen me and help me. He will uphold me (Author paraphrase).

Philippians 4:13—

My God supplies all of my need according to His riches in glory.

1 Corinthians 2:16—

I have the mind of Christ.

John 10:27—

I hear the voice of the Good Shepherd and follow His voice.
The stranger's voice I will not follow (Author paraphrase).

Hebrews 3:7—

Today, I will hear what the Holy Spirit is saying (Author paraphrase).

2 Corinthians 10:4–5—

I cast down every imagination of thought that exalts itself
against the knowledge of God and His Word. I bring every
thought captive to the obedience of God's Word (Author paraphrase).

Philippians 4:8—

I think on things that are true, honest, just, pure, lovely, and
of good report. I think about things that are good and praise-
worthy (Author paraphrase).

Romans 8:14—

I choose to be led by the Spirit (Author paraphrase).

1 Corinthians 15:57—

Thanks be to God, who gives me victory through my Lord
Jesus Christ (Author paraphrase).

2 Corinthians 2:14—

He always causes me to triumph in Christ and uses me to spread the knowledge of Christ everywhere, like a sweet perfume (Author paraphrase).

1 John 4:4—

I am God's child, and I have overcome the antichrist spirit; for greater is He that is in me than he that is in the world (Author paraphrase).

Acts 17:28—

In Him I live and move and have my being (Author paraphrase).

2 Timothy 1:7—

God has not given me the spirit of fear, but of power, love, and a sound mind (Author paraphrase).

Proverbs 3:5–6—

I trust in the LORD *with all my heart. I lean not on my own understanding. In all my ways I acknowledge Him and He will direct my path* (Author paraphrase).

Psalm 91 (NKJV)—

He who dwells in the secret place of the Most High shall abide under the shadow of the Almighty.

"I will say of the LORD, *'He is my refuge and my fortress; my God, in Him I will trust.'"*

"Surely He shall deliver me from the snare of the fowler and from the perilous pestilence.

"He shall cover me with His feathers, and under His wings I shall take refuge; His truth shall be my shield and buckler.

"I shall not be afraid of the terror by night, nor of the arrow that flies by day,

"Nor of the pestilence that walks in darkness, nor of the destruction that lays waste at noonday.

"A thousand may fall at my side, and ten thousand at my right hand; but it shall not come near me.

"Only with my eyes shall I look, and see the reward of the wicked.

"Because I have made the LORD, *who is my refuge, even the Most High, my dwelling place,*

"No evil shall befall me, nor shall any plague come near my dwelling;

"For He shall give His angels charge over me, to keep me in all my ways.

"In their hands they shall bear me up, lest I dash my foot against a stone.

"I shall tread upon the lion and the cobra, the young lion and the serpent I shall trample underfoot.

"Because I have has set my love upon Him, therefore He will deliver me; He will set me on high, because I have known His name.

"I shall call upon Him, and He will answer me; He will be with me in trouble; He will deliver me and honor me.

"With long life He will satisfy me, and show me His salvation" (Author paraphrase).

Meditating and speaking Scripture bring a greater awareness of God's presence helping you. When we talk about being aware of

God's presence with us continually, it is an attitude and mind-set of faith. It is accepting God's promises and speaking what He says instead of living by your feelings and emotions. Your emotions can be like a yo-yo—up and down—but when you choose to accept God's promises and act on them, you bring your emotions and feelings into submission to God's Word. You let your spirit dominate your mind, emotions, and feelings.

The Rock, Jesus Christ, Is Your Defense

Believe me, I understand how thoughts and emotions will try to overwhelm you at times. We all have to bring our thoughts and emotions captive. The psalmist said, "When my heart is overwhelmed; lead me to the rock that is higher than I" (Psalm 61:2, NKJV). The rock symbolizes stability, something that will not be moved. The rock that is higher than you or me is God Himself. Psalm 62:6 tells us, "He only is my rock and my salvation; He is my defense; I shall not be moved" (NKJV).

In my own life I've seen God's help supernaturally. I've also been grateful for those around me who have felt responsible to help me and to defend me. Even apart from the church, God has sent help to me at times when I needed it. I have always believed the scripture in Hebrews 7:25 that says Jesus intercedes for me continually, and I also believe my husband, who is now in heaven, prays for me still. Hebrews 12:1 indicates that there is a great cloud of witnesses surrounding us, and I believe they are praying for us as well.

It is a great comfort and encouragement to know that God is with me. I do not have to fear the future. Even when I cannot see everything ahead, I know He is not only with me, but He is also for me (see Romans 8:31).

What Happens When You Are Assured of God's Presence?

When you know God is with you:

1. You do not have to fear the future.

2. You do not have to fear others.

3. You do not have to compare yourself with others, but instead you can be who God created you to be.

4. You can do whatever God says.

5. You can know He will instruct you and counsel you.

6. You can know He will surround you like a shield and give you favor.

7. You can know you can overcome whatever challenges lie ahead of you.

8. You can know He will defend you.

9. You can know He will strengthen you.

10. You can know He will work things together for good.

Just like you, I have to remind myself that God is with me, and as my husband used to say, He will help me do "the right thing at the right time and in the right way" as I keep my trust in Him.

I've had my moments of feeling less than able, but I know I have to speak to myself what God says instead of my feelings. Praying in tongues and speaking Scripture continue to get me back in faith.

> *My help comes from the* LORD, *who made heaven and earth.*
> *He will not let you be defeated. He who guards you never sleeps.*
> *He who guards Israel never rests or sleeps.*
> *The* LORD *guards you. The* LORD *is the shade that protects you from the sun.*
> *The sun cannot hurt you during the day, and the moon cannot hurt you at night.*
> *The* LORD *will protect you from all dangers; he will guard your life.*
> *The* LORD *will guard you as you come and go, both now and forever.*
>
> —PSALM 121:2–8, NCV

Chapter 9

PRAYER

"Draw near to God, and he will draw near to you..." (James 4:8, Darby). You have an open phone connection with heaven anytime, all the time.

Someone said to me, "How can you continue to pray when you didn't see your prayer answered the way you believed it would be answered?"

My answer is that prayer is like breathing. We need to breathe to live. I need my prayer relationship with God like I need to breathe. That's because God is not my problem. He is my help, and He gives me His counsel and grace to live my life with purpose.

Prayer is you talking to God and God talking to you in thoughts that He speaks to your heart. It's good to have a time you set aside to pray each day and to read Scripture. Then it's important to keep a consciousness of His voice speaking to you throughout the day.

Some might say, "Well, how do you know it is God talking to your thoughts?" God always says things that agree with His written Word. His Word is our measuring standard to discern our thoughts.

When thoughts come to your mind in prayer, you know when they line up with God's written Word, and you recognize that it is His voice. Otherwise, they are simply your own thoughts. Hebrews

4:12 says that God's Word discerns our thoughts. His Word divides between what is coming from our own soulish desires and reasoning and what is coming from God to our spirit.

The Draw of Heaven to Know Jesus

Realizing there is a draw of heaven upon our lives, it is obvious that God not only wants us to enter the door of salvation, but He wants us to grow in a relationship with Him. He always wants to draw us higher than where we are at the present moment.

How do we go higher? Isaiah 55:9 says, "As the heavens are higher than the earth, so are My ways higher than your ways, and My thoughts than your thoughts." God reveals His thoughts and His ways to us in His Word. The more you go to the Word and read it, meditate it, and let it speak to you, the more you will begin to think from God's perspective instead of from your natural reasoning.

He can settle the questioning in your heart of "why?" and He can help you let go of doubt, fear, and disappointment.

First of all, we need to realize that our loved one is in a blessed place. He or she is experiencing the glory of God's presence and the beauty of heaven. However, we see circumstances around us and sometimes think about the drastic change or difficulties his passing may have created.

Emotions can cause a person to blame people or blame God. Sometimes people can only see the moment they are in, but God sees beyond the moment. He sees a future and a hope for you and me. (See Jeremiah 29:11.) He sees how He can cause people to grow into greater strength. He sees people He wants to connect with your life.

Some will help you, while you will help others. He sees that where you have been dependent upon that loved one in the past to fulfill your needs, now He wants to draw you to Him so He can fulfill your needs.

When a loved one dies and you begin to take time to sit, read, and meditate on the Word of God, He draws you to minister into the depths of your soul. In this place of waiting upon the Lord, you will begin to hear His voice inside your heart, giving you direction. His Holy Spirit will speak into your thoughts. I found that when I didn't know exactly what to pray that my prayer language of the Spirit (praying in tongues) gave me peace and strengthened me.

Many years ago a friend of ours, Terry Law (who is over World Compassion Ministries), received a phone call while he was overseas ministering. He was told that his wife had been killed in a car accident. Obviously, it was a shock to him. He rushed back to his children and began the process of managing and balancing family and ministry responsibilities.

Brother Oral Roberts met with Terry and said, "Terry, you've got to pray in your prayer language of the Spirit. Pray in tongues." Brother Roberts told Terry that when he and Evelyn had experienced the death of an adult daughter and son-in-law, and later their oldest son who died, it was praying in tongues that helped them emotionally, mentally, and spiritually to continue to go forward. Terry said it was true. As he prayed in the Spirit, the Holy Spirit took over and kept him, and he heard God's direction concerning things he had to do.

Heaven draws us to receive help in our time of need. When we respond to that calling in seeking Him, we move into a supernatural grace that envelops us and carries us forward.

The night of my husband's passing, we had been praying in the Spirit, worshiping God and speaking Scripture in prayer around Billy Joe's bed and playing a healing CD as well. When he passed, I continued to pray for his resurrection, worshiping God, and speaking the Word of God, which I did for a little over three hours. I know Hebrews 11:35 gave me the scriptural basis to do this. Looking at the smile on his face, however, I knew that Billy Joe had passed into eternity with Jesus and had entered into his rest. I knew he was happy.

After his passing, my head was foggy, but my heart was still connected with God. Later, it seemed that praying in tongues was such a release in my spirit, because I could just let the Holy Spirit pray through me since my own mind and words were so limited.

Romans 8:26–27 (NASB) says:

> *The Spirit also helps our weakness; for we do not know how to pray as we should, but the Spirit Himself intercedes for us with groanings too deep for words; and He who searches the hearts knows what the mind of the Spirit is, because He intercedes for the saints according to the will of God.*

The word *helps* here in the Greek is *sunantilambano,* which means the Holy Spirit connects with you or partners with you to pray. The word *weakness* in the Greek is *astheneia,* which describes someone weak or broken in their mind and emotions who needs help because of not knowing just how to pray at the moment.

The Holy Spirit prays through us beyond our own reasoning and understanding. He searches deep within a person, and He also knows the will of God and prays accordingly. The word *intercede* in the Greek is *huperentugchano,* which means to take over and rescue you in praying what is needed. The Holy Spirit helps to rescue us in praying what is needed when we don't know at the present what to do or how to pray about a situation.

When we pray in tongues, the Holy Spirit intercedes or prays through us and prays for us the will of God. Think about that. When we pray in tongues, we cooperate with the Holy Spirit as He intercedes for us. At the same time, He builds up our spirit.

Jude wrote in verse 20 (NKJV), "But you, beloved, building yourselves up on your most holy faith, praying in the Holy Spirit." I needed to be built up in my spirit and in my faith, trusting in God. Faith is not only believing for something, but faith is also having a belief that trusts in God in the midst of difficult circumstances.

As I prayed in the Spirit and in my understanding, God began to speak to my thoughts regarding His direction in my life. I heard Him speak certain scriptures to me, and I heard Him say that my purpose had not changed, nor had my calling.

He then spoke to me a word to get up and "steady the ship"—to move forward—as I mentioned earlier. That had to be God and not my own head, because had I reasoned with it, it might have seemed overwhelming or questionable to some. Prayer is what led me to trust God, and prayer continues to lead me to trust God.

Prayer is simply about a relationship between you and God. What a wonderful blessing it was for me to know that there were enough other believers who were praying as well who supported me and rose to steady the ship with me. I had to have others around me because God knew I needed their giftings and abilities to help me.

I believe this prayer relationship with God keeps us from the enemy's devices that sometimes try to divide people. The late Edwin Louis Cole, founder of the Christian Men's Network and a prolific author and speaker, often said, "Prayer produces unity." The Holy Spirit kept us in unity. I'm so grateful for a united staff who prayed and remained united.

As I mentioned before, following my husband's passing, that very night a friend of ours was scheduled to speak at our church, and instead of teaching or preaching, he led a prayer meeting and a time of worship. We have had other prayer and worship services since that time. I believe worship and prayer brought healing to those who participated, especially in those first months.

Later, when I saw other people who were not a part of these worship and prayer gatherings, I noticed that they still struggled over my husband's passing. I know that my husband would have wanted people to be strong and stand together. He believed that, through prayer, worship, fellowship with others, and meditating the Word of God, God enables people to rise above grief over time and go forward with His plans.

Praying in the Spirit

Whenever you are going through any painful situation and it is difficult to think clearly, praying in tongues bypasses your mind and supernaturally brings you inner strength.

The Apostle Paul wrote in 1 Corinthians 14:15 (AMPC):

> *I will pray with my spirit [by the Holy Spirit that is within me], but I will also pray [intelligently] with my mind and*

understanding; I will sing with my spirit [by the Holy Spirit that is within me], but I will sing [intelligently] with my mind and understanding also.

It is not easy when a loved one dies. Sometimes it can feel painful. But praying in tongues can ease the pain, and the Holy Spirit can not only comfort you, but He can also speak to your heart what you need at the moment.

Understanding the Holy Spirit

The Holy Spirit comes to live within a person when they accept Jesus as Lord and Savior. First Corinthians 12:3 (NKJV) says, "No one can say that Jesus is Lord except by the Holy Spirit." John 3:5–8 records that Jesus said that when we are born again, we are born of the Spirit.

Jesus told His disciples, after He had been resurrected and appeared to them, to go to Jerusalem to an upper room where they would receive the promise of God and be endued with (or clothed with) power from on high (see Luke 24:49). Jesus referred to it as being baptized with the Holy Spirit.

We can drink in the Holy Spirit when we are born again (John 7:37). However, when we understand that the baptism of the Holy Spirit is like a ship being submerged in water, we are filled in and out. The baptism of the Holy Spirit was to empower believers who believe that Jesus can work through their lives with supernatural signs, wonders, and miracles as they share the gospel message. The baptism of the Holy Spirit releases the rivers of living water out of your innermost being.

In Acts 1:5 and 8 (NKJV) Jesus said, "John truly baptized with water, but you shall be baptized with the Holy Spirit not many days from now...But you shall receive power when the Holy Spirit has come upon you; and you shall be witnesses to Me in Jerusalem, and in all Judea and Samaria, and to the end of the earth."

There were 120 believers gathered together at that time—men and women—when the Holy Spirit was first poured out in Acts 2. These believers began speaking in other tongues as the Holy Spirit gave them the languages. They went out in the streets, where Jews had come from various nations of the earth, speaking in their languages the wonderful works of God.

The crowd was amazed because they knew these people, being uneducated, did not know how to speak in their languages, and yet they were speaking fluently to them. Some said, "These men are full of new wine" (Acts 2:13). Peter, who had been fearful before, stood up and preached that this was the fulfillment of Joel 2:28–29, that in the last days God said He would pour out His Spirit on all flesh— sons and daughters, old and young, men and women.

Then he said that the gift of the Holy Spirit was given to all who would repent and be baptized for the remission of sins and that this gift was for people, even in the future beyond that moment (Acts 2:17–39).

Throughout the book of Acts, we see believers receiving the baptism of the Holy Spirit with the evidence of speaking in tongues (see Acts 8:14–17; 19:1–6).

When Peter was told by the Lord to go to Cornelius's house and speak, he went. And as he was speaking, the Holy Spirit fell upon those listening, and they began to speak with other tongues because they believed his message that he preached about Jesus. (See Acts 10:44–46.)

All the New Testament writers had this experience. Paul, who was not present on the day of Pentecost, said in 1 Corinthians 14:18 (NKJV), "I thank my God I speak with tongues more than you all." Isaiah foresaw this gift: "For with stammering lips and another tongue He will speak to this people, to whom He said, 'This is the rest with which You may cause the weary to rest,' and 'This is the refreshing...'" (Isaiah 28:11–12, NKJV).

As I said earlier, when you receive Jesus into your heart, the Holy Spirit comes in. However, there is an enduement of His power as well. I found that it was simply releasing the river of God that was already within me as I began to pray in other tongues for the first time.

It seemed at first as if I were stammering, and then it began to pour out of me. I wept and then I began to laugh. I was oblivious to other people while I was praying at an altar. The denomination I was raised in did not practice this experience, so everything was new to me.

After this, I found that praying in tongues helped me in so many ways:

1. The Holy Spirit could pray through me when I didn't know exactly what to pray in my own understanding. (See Romans 8:26–27.)

2. As I prayed in tongues, I would get built up inside. (See Jude 20 and 1 Corinthians 14:4.)

3.   I found that praying in tongues brought thoughts to
      my mind about situations that I didn't know in my
      own knowledge, and later I'd find out it was right.
      This is revelation knowledge. (See 1 Corinthians 14:2
      and John 16:13.)

4.   Praying in tongues sharpened my discernment as well.
      (See 1 Corinthians 2:9–16.)

5.   Praying in the Spirit was a spiritual renewing and
      refreshing to my mind. (See Isaiah 28:11–12.)

6.   Praying in tongues built up my faith to believe God
      could work miracles in my life and use me to inspire
      others to believe for miracles. (See Jude 20; Mark
      16:17–18.)

It might surprise you, but we must contend for God's supernatural power no matter what experiences we have walked through in this life. People need God's supernatural power and divine messengers and carriers of His power and saving grace.

Steps to Releasing the Supernatural Gift of the Holy Spirit

When you ask the Lord to fill you to overflowing with His Spirit, He will. (See Luke 11:9–13.) Believe you receive when you pray. (See Mark 11:24.) Then, by faith, open your mouth and let God fill it. (See Psalm 81:10.)

The Bible says that the disciples began to speak with other tongues as the Spirit gave them utterance. (See Acts 2:4.) Notice the phrase, "[They] began to speak with other tongues…" (v. 4). Begin to speak whatever the Holy Spirit prompts you to speak. Worship and thank God. Begin to move from your known language to an unknown language.

The spirit of a person is subject to that person. This means you won't be walking down a street and all of a sudden uncontrollably start speaking in tongues. You have the ability to pray in tongues or not pray in tongues. The wonderful thing is that you can pray in tongues if you desire to and believe. Mark 16:17 says this is one of the signs that will follow a believer. Of course, this means that it will follow you if you believe it will follow you.

I realize that not every Christian speaks in tongues. However, this gift is invaluable to every believer. I have personally found that this gift has moved me into a realm of God's supernatural help and strength that I could not have had otherwise. His power is released in our lives when we pray in tongues. Faith rises in our hearts when we pray in tongues to believe for the supernatural of God.

Ephesians 6:18 (NLT) says to "pray in the Spirit at all times and on every occasion. Stay alert and be persistent in your prayers for all believers everywhere." When Paul wrote for us to "pray in the Spirit," he was speaking about praying in tongues. In 1 Corinthians 14:15 (NKJV) he wrote, "I will pray with the spirit, and I will also pray with the understanding. I will sing with the spirit, and I will also sing with the understanding."

We have reason to believe that, along with knowing the Old Testament prophetic scriptures, praying in the Spirit enabled Paul to write half of the New Testament books. Remember, he wasn't around Jesus physically. He wasn't one of the original twelve disciples. He came along after the fact. How did he end up writing half of the books of the New Testament? He is the one who taught us about praying in the Spirit and praying for the interpretation. He said, "I became a minister according to the gift of the grace of God given to me by the effective working of His power" (Ephesians 3:7, NKJV). In other words, "I didn't get these things from man. I got them by revelation from the Holy Spirit." (See Ephesians 3:3.)

Revelation is going to come to you from the Holy Spirit regarding the steps you need to take and the things you need to do in the days ahead. Thank God for His Holy Spirit and guidance from heaven. Sometimes people wonder, "What am I going to do?" You have GPS—God's Positioning System—inside of your heart. God will position you.

Jeremiah 33:3 (WEB) says, "Call to me, and I will answer you, and will show you great things, and difficult, which you don't know."

Prayer is powerful. Never underestimate what prayer can accomplish. James 5:16 (NIV) says that "the prayer of a righteous person is powerful and effective."

When we pray in the Spirit and we pray Scripture by His guidance, God releases heaven's help (angels) to assist us. (See Hebrews 1:14 and Psalm 103:20.) We give our voice to God's Word as we pray, and the angels hearken to that Word to help us.

Years ago, one of our church staff members, a single mom, shared with me that she was at our church prayer room praying in tongues one night. She had committed to pray each week at the time for various needs at the church and requests of our congregation. Afterward, she felt that she and her son should not go home immediately. They stayed about forty minutes longer and walked on our school track as they prayed.

When they arrived at their apartment, police were there and had busted up a drug situation in the apartment next to theirs. There had been a person shooting a gun. The police said that it was good that she and her son were not there forty minutes earlier. They had avoided the whole scenario. That is just one story of praying in the Spirit and, as a result, its supernatural help to our lives.

If you have not experienced the baptism of the Holy Spirit, I would encourage you to pray this prayer right now, asking the Father to baptize you with the Holy Spirit. Believe that you receive when you pray; then begin to worship the Lord. As the Spirit prays through you, you will experience His supernatural presence flooding your life.

> Father, I come to You in the name of Jesus. I have been born again as a result of the work of the cross where Jesus made provision for salvation for all who would receive Him.
>
> I am totally surrendered to Your will for my life, and I now ask You, Lord Jesus, to baptize me with Your Holy Spirit so that I can pray in other tongues and receive Your supernatural power and help in my life.
>
> Thank You, Jesus, for filling me with Your Holy Spirit and releasing Your river of life out of my heart in praise and worship to You. Amen.

When Things Don't Go As You Planned

I want to encourage you not to keep looking back. Sometimes, as in our situation, when we and many other people prayed and did not see what we had wanted to see happen, some people lost confidence in praying. Just as you don't stop breathing, don't stop praying. Jesus said in Luke 18:1–8 that we should always pray and not faint.

Dake's Bible says "to not lose heart; not give in to doubt, fear, unbelief, or discouragement." Then Jesus said in Luke 18:8 (AMP): "When the Son of Man comes, will He find [this kind of persistent] faith on the earth?"[10]

"Persistence" is to continue steadfastly or firmly in a course of action and purpose in spite of opposition. It is to carry on in prayer and in faith.

When we continue to pray, we continue to keep our faith going. Prayer is our communication line with heaven. Keep talking to God, and keep your heart open to hear Him speak back into your life.

---

10 Ibid.

Chapter 10

WORSHIP

I'VE ALWAYS LOVED THE SONG, "Turn Your Eyes Upon Jesus." "Look full in His wonderful face, and the things of earth will grow strangely dim in the light of His glory and grace."

These words capture the essence of worship. When we close our eyes and imagine ourselves standing before the Lord, lifting our hands to the One who created us, the One who loves us, and the One who can supply all that we need, everything around us becomes settled and at peace. That is how we set our affection upon the things above and not on the things below as Colossians 3:1 says.

"O God, my heart is fixed; I will sing and give praise, even with my glory." (See Psalm 108:1.) Another version says, "My heart is steady. I will sing and praise you with all my being" (NCV). My heart is *fixed* as I worship the Lord. The word *fixed* means "settled, established, firm, stable, not subject to change."

The psalmist had a personal heart-to-heart relationship with God. When you read the Psalms, you are reading his prayers and his songs of worship. Many times he states his faith in God in spite of his difficult circumstances.

Worship is the key to heaven's presence enveloping you and giving you supernatural strength that goes beyond your mind's reasoning. Worship draws upon God's glory, filling your life and covering you.

Psalm 84:4–7 (AMP) says:

> *Blessed and greatly favored are those who dwell in Your house and Your presence; they will be singing Your praises all the day long. Selah.*
>
> *Blessed and greatly favored is the man whose strength is in You, in whose heart are the highways to Zion.*
>
> *Passing through the Valley of Weeping (Baca), they make it a place of springs; the early rain also covers it with blessings.*
>
> *They go from strength to strength [increasing in victorious power]; each of them appears before God in Zion.*

Through the years I've come to realize that worship and prayer go hand in hand. Worship is prayer in song. Worship, however, gets prayer off the ground because worship expresses our faith that God hears and responds to us.

I believe the psalmist got a revelation of worship that enabled him to rise above disappointment, depression, fear, and any other negative thoughts from the devil. Worship focuses your thoughts upon the One who loves you, who created you, and who will defend, deliver, and empower you.

In worship you are acknowledging that you are absolutely dependent upon God, like a child with his or her father. You believe that as you draw to Him with your heart and with your thoughts, He draws to you with His thoughts, speaking into your heart. (See James 4:8.)

True Worship

In John 4, Jesus was at a well, and a woman came to draw water. He started the conversation by asking her for a drink. She was surprised that He, as a Jew, was speaking to her, because she was a Samaritan and Jews didn't converse with Samaritans. A Jewish man certainly wouldn't speak to a non-Jewish woman.

He told her He had water and if she drank it, she would never thirst again. She wanted this water, so Jesus said to go get her husband. She said she didn't have a husband. He then affirmed her statement and said she was right in that she had had five husbands and was living with a man who wasn't her husband.

I thought about this story. Not only was she convicted of her sin of not being married to the man she was living with, but Jesus was trying to help her see that her fulfillment and identity were not in a man. She had been searching for life in relationships with men. Jesus was helping her see that her identity and fulfillment in life were in knowing God and having a personal relationship with Him.

She changed the subject to talk about worship, and Jesus explained that worship is about having a relationship with God—worshiping Him from your spirit because He is a Spirit. He seeks those who understand our entire lives are to be about worshiping Him.

Jesus said, "True worshipers will worship the Father in spirit and truth; *for the Father is seeking such to worship Him.* God is Spirit, and those who worship Him must worship in spirit and truth" (John 4:23–24, NKJV, author's emphasis).

When Jesus said that those who worship God must worship in spirit and truth, He meant that worship was to be from the heart, with an attitude of love and genuineness or honesty with God. Worship is not just about words we've learned to say mechanically, but words to which our hearts are connected.

Worship affects your attitude, your conversation with others, and what you do.

Worship isn't just about singing songs, although He loves for us to sing to Him. Singing is part of it. Worship is about honoring God with how we live our lives. Either we bring Him honor or dishonor. Worship is about where we find our identity and our fulfillment. When we find Him, then we look to Him as our Source for living. Instead of feeling that we can't live without a person, we see that we can't live without the Lord and all that He is to us.

No matter what we may face in life—tests, disappointments, pain, failure, or any adversity—our love for God and our need to be able to open our heart to the One who loves us and understands us most, should never change. Worship is the ability to draw to God and allow Him to draw to us.

There are amazing songs of worship that have been written through the years by people who have been able to put their words to music, and who have found the overcoming strength they needed in their own tests. God has used these songs to help many others.

I know in my own walk with the Lord, especially in overcoming my husband's passing, the Holy Spirit would bring to my mind and heart worship songs at various moments that I've learned over the years. There were certain worship songs that Billy Joe loved to listen to and to sing right before his passing that are still dear to my heart—songs we sang at his memorial service.

In Billy Joe's earlier years in ministry, he didn't express his worship in dancing. I was the one who seemed to be less inhibited to express my emotions in worship through dancing, clapping, lifting my hands, etc. However, through the years, I watched Billy Joe get freed up and more uninhibited to even dance unto the Lord.

In those last few weeks before his passing, as weak as he was physically, there would be moments when he'd get up and dance, waving his hands and singing the song, "Wonderful God." Then he'd sit in his chair and with tears flowing down his face, he'd sing, "Worshiping You": "I'm Gonna Worship You Forever, I'm Gonna Worship You." Even today these songs bring back those memories to my mind when we sing them in church.

I believe when people walk through circumstances where they have time alone with God, they are able to see what is more valuable in life. They view things with eternity in mind. In my own life, I've found that so many things don't matter that people sometimes get hung up with.

Surrender in Worship

Another aspect about worship is surrender. I remember when, many years ago, my husband shared from Genesis 22 about Abraham's worship. God had supernaturally blessed Abraham and Sarah in their old age with a child named Isaac. God said it would be through Isaac that He would establish His covenant with Abraham and that Isaac's seed would be through which He would multiply. (See Genesis 17.)

However, in Genesis 22 God told Abraham to take his only son Isaac to offer him as a burnt offering on Mount Moriah. Abraham took Isaac on a donkey and two young men with them to the mountain. He left the two young men at the base of the mountain, and said to them, "Stay here with the donkey while I and the boy go over there. We will worship and then we will come back to you" (Genesis 22:5, NIV).

Abraham believed that God would keep His promise concerning Isaac, and that even if Isaac would become a burnt offering, God would raise him from the dead and fulfill His promise. Abraham believed that he and his son Isaac would return to the two young men. (See Genesis 17:19.)

Isaac asked his father where the lamb for the offering was. Abraham replied that God Himself would provide the lamb for the offering. However, Abraham went ahead to prepare the wood and bound his son as he laid Isaac on the altar. As he lifted his knife, the angel of the Lord stepped in and said, "Abraham! Abraham!...Do not lay a hand on the boy...Do not do anything to him. Now I know that you fear God, because you have not withheld from me your son, your only son" (Genesis 22:11–12, NIV).

The Lord then had a ram caught in a bush to be offered as an offering. God said, "I will surely bless you and make your descendants as numerous as the stars in the sky and as the sand on the seashore. Your descendants will take possession of the cities of their enemies, and through your offspring all nations on earth will be blessed, because you have obeyed me" (Genesis 22:17–18, NIV).

This account is all about worship. There were no tambourines, guitars, keyboards, drums, or horns. The worship was about total surrender and obedience to God.

Worship is not just about music. That's a wonderful part of worship, but worship is about surrendering your heart to God and obeying Him when it costs you something. It may seem hard at first, but the reward is so much greater.

God has given me fulfillment in doing His will. I've also been able to see so many lives changed and impacted because of doing what He says. I've experienced His grace in pressing through difficult times, such as ministering in funeral services or ministering in settings that Billy Joe and I did together in the past.

God has allowed me to see people healed of diseases as I've prayed with them for miracles. There is no greater fulfillment than living in surrender to the Lord.

A Life of Worship

Worship really encompasses how we live our lives, what we live for, and who we live for. One day, as believers, we will step from earth into heaven. It will be determined in eternity whether or not we understood worship here on earth. The circumstances on earth that we walk through do not change our worship. Our worship continues to develop and grow as we know the Lord more.

"Therefore by Him let us continually offer the sacrifice of praise to God, that is, the fruit of our lips, giving thanks to His name" (Hebrews 13:15, NKJV).

Praise is a tremendous resource that brings healing. The Bible says again and again to praise God. This means to worship, honor, and thank Him. Even when you do not feel like praising God, do it because you believe in the power of praise. Praising God when it hurts and when it costs you something will bring breakthrough in your life. It may cost you emotionally, letting go of heartache and pain. It may cost you logic or reasoning. It may cost you in traditions of how others around you have always thought you should grieve. It may cost you time in going to church to be with others in worshiping or changing your lifestyle. God sees this sacrifice of praise, and He responds with meeting your deepest need.

The Bible says to offer the "sacrifice of praise" to God with lips that thankfully acknowledge, confess, and proclaim the glory of His name. Your healing is intertwined in praise.

Praise and worship release your heart and soul from the pain of grief and adversity. God inhabits the praises of His people. Make the effort to go to worship gatherings to worship with others. Being with others worshiping God brings healing and freedom to your emotions.

Even when you are still emotionally raw, worship goes deep within your soul to release your spirit, and in that place God will not only bring His supernatural healing and comfort; but He will speak His thoughts into your heart. Everything God is will minister to you in that place of communion with Him.

"But thou art holy, O thou that inhabitest the praises of Israel" (Psalm 22:3). God not only comes to live within our hearts, but when we worship, God comes down to inhabit our praise. Everything He is comes to our aid.

Psalm 34:1 says, "I will bless the Lord at all times: his praise shall continually be in my mouth." "At all times" means "at all times."

Think about the psalmist David. In 2 Samuel 12:20, David had been fasting and praying for the life of his baby that he had with

Bathsheba. David had committed adultery with her and had her husband killed in battle so he could marry her. David repented, and when the baby was born, it was very sick. David earnestly prayed, but the baby died.

When he heard the news about the baby's death, his servants thought he might be plunged into depression and grief. However, instead he arose and washed himself. He anointed himself and went to the temple to worship God. His servants were amazed.

He told them, "While the child was alive, I fasted and wept; for I said, 'Who can tell whether the LORD will be gracious to me, that the child may live?' But now he is dead; why should I fast? Can I bring him back again? I shall go to him, but he shall not return to me" (2 Samuel 12:22–23, NKJV).

David had an understanding of eternity and heaven. He also had an understanding of God's love. He believed that God loved him and God loved his baby. He knew that he had sinned, and though the child had been born sick, he believed his repentance could bring God's mercy in spite of the circumstances. This was why he fasted and prayed.

Psalm 51 describes David's repentance and his faith in God's mercy and love. Scripture shows us David's relationship with God was all about his understanding of worship.

David was not a perfect person, but he believed God, and he knew that the greatest thing in his life was his relationship with God. He knew his relationship with God would bring healing and enable him to continue to live in God's purpose. Acts 13:36 (AMPC) later records, "For David, after he had served God's will and purpose and counsel in his own generation, fell asleep [in death] and was buried among his forefathers...."

David went through many troubling times in his life here on earth, but in all of his troubles, he didn't let his failures stop him from seeking God through worship and prayer. He found a place of worship and spent time with God, his Father, talking to Him, listening to Him, singing, playing his harp, writing songs God gave him, and speaking to others about God's Word and His love (Psalm 56:4, 9–10; 63:3–4, NKJV). Even to this day, Israel considers David their greatest king. Jesus Himself came through the lineage of David.

Our praise and worship takes our minds off of the difficulties and places our thoughts on the Lord who will strengthen us and keep us in the days to come.

Chapter 11

HEAVEN SPEAKS TO US IN DREAMS AND VISIONS

And it shall come to pass in the last days, saith God, I will pour out of my Spirit upon all flesh: and your sons and your daughters shall prophesy, and your young men shall see visions, and your old men shall dream dreams:

And on my servants and on my handmaidens I will pour out in those days of my Spirit; and they shall prophesy:

And I will shew wonders in heaven above, and signs in the earth beneath....

—Acts 2:17–19
Joel 2:28–29

For God speaks once, yes twice,
yet man does not perceive it.

In a dream, in a vision of the night,
when deep sleep falls upon men,
in slumber on their beds,

then He opens the ears of men,
and seals their instruction.

—Job 33:14–16, mev

I N BOTH THE OLD Testament and in the New Testament, we see how at various times God has spoken to people through dreams or visions. Sometimes He gave dreams or visions to reveal Himself to people (Acts 9:10–12; 26:13–19; 7:55–56). Sometimes it was to tell His plans in using people (Luke 1:11–20, 26–38). At other times dreams or visions were to give warning or tell of things to come (Genesis 15:12–21; Daniel, chapters 8–12; Revelation, chapters 6–22). Then there have been times He has used dreams and visions to give direction or simply to affirm those whom He had called for His purposes (Acts 10:1–6, 9–22; 16:9; 18:9).

Walking out visions and dreams was a large part of our lives together from the moment Billy Joe and I began our marriage and ministry together.

There are three kinds of visions:

1. The natural visual sight of the eyes.

2. The natural imagination that is used to think and see beyond what things look like. It is to think creatively. It is to have foresight and think of what could be done to prepare for something. It is to use the imagination to create solutions for problems, such as the discovery of electricity or flying a plane or making a car or telephone, etc.

3. Supernatural visions and dreams from God is where someone has an experience seeing something vividly appearing to the mind that is not actually present. It is to see something supernaturally that the person hasn't been thinking about. It is to see something

supernaturally and suddenly from God that God will use to fulfill His Word and will. God speaks many times in dreams while we sleep.

There are two kinds of supernatural visions:

1. An open vision—When someone hears from God and sees something by the Spirit of God, but they are awake and aware of their surroundings.

2. A closed vision—Where someone hears from God and sees something by the Spirit of God, but they are in a type of trance, *or* they are asleep and they are unaware of the surroundings around them. A dream in the night would also be in the category of a closed vision.

God's dreams and visions are never to create confusion or to terrify us with no hope. Remember, He is the God of all hope. He doesn't give dreams and visions to make us feel helpless either. He desires to be our help in time of need. He does give dreams and visions to help us see beyond what we know with our natural understanding at times. He gives visions to help us realize that He can work supernaturally when things look impossible because He loves us (Genesis, chapters 37–50; Acts 27:23).

God Uses Dreams to Speak to Us Today

We live in a world where there are many distractions around us. Sometimes it is when we sleep that we are still enough for God to speak to us. There have been times through the years that I have had a dream or been awakened hearing God speak to my thoughts. I have also had times when I was seeking God, and I saw in my mind a direction from God in a vision that helped me do the right thing at that moment. I can remember dreams that warned me about something and dreams when I was encouraged about something.

I also know that not every dream comes from God. I would imagine that we have all had crazy dreams or even scary dreams that left us uneasy or with no answer or insight. Possibly you ate something that night before going to bed that caused unrestful sleep, or you watched something on TV or someone said something that lodged in your subconscious that attributed to the dream you had. Sometimes bad dreams are a result of bad experiences that have happened in life, and the enemy seeks to torment a person with them.

The point I am making is that not every dream is from God, even though sometimes God speaks to us in our dreams. God can cover our minds and emotions when we sleep if we let Him. What we meditate on is important. When we read and take time to meditate on the Word of God, when we listen to worship music, or when we pray in the Spirit, our hearts are more open to God's voice.

An important factor is being able to discern our dreams. I believe when we are seeking God daily in His Word and in prayer, it enables us to be in tune with God's Holy Spirit so that we can hear the voice of the Good Shepherd and recognize the stranger's voice (John 10:4–5, 27; Hebrews 4:12; John 16:13).

I realize there are other voices around us that we have to discern. First Corinthians 14:10 says, "There are, it may be, so many kinds of voices in the world...." We still live in a world where we have an enemy who seeks to interrupt our thoughts at times. This requires us to keep a guard over our hearts, our minds, and our emotions.

God Spoke Through Visions

A vision can come to a person while he or she is awake. God speaks to us at times in visions while we are awake to give us direction, understanding, to show us things to come, to encourage us, or to bring an answer to prayer. I have found that this happens at times in a state of prayer and meditation on God's Word.

In Acts 10:9 we read how Peter was praying and went into a trance where he saw a vision from God one day while waiting on lunch that was being prepared. He had gone to a place alone to pray. Suddenly he saw a vision of a sheet with all kinds of animals coming down from heaven and he heard a voice say, "Kill, and eat" (v. 13). Peter responded that he didn't eat certain meats because they were unclean according to the law God gave to Moses. But he heard God say, "Don't call unclean what I have called clean." (See vv. 14–15.)

After he saw this in a vision three times, he heard the Holy Spirit say to go with the Gentile men who were coming at that moment to the house where he was staying. When they arrived, Peter went with them to Cornelius's house and preached about Jesus. If he had not had that vision, he would not have gone with non-Jewish people, especially people he had never met before.

Cornelius was a Gentile who prayed to the God of Abraham, Isaac, and Jacob; and he had given money to many poor Jews.

Cornelius had had an open vision the day before as he was praying and saw an angel appear who spoke to him that God had heard his prayers and saw his giving; and he was to send men to Joppa to find a man named Peter who would speak to him and his household and tell him what he was to do.

While Peter spoke to the people gathered at Cornelius's house, the Holy Spirit was poured out upon those listening, and they spoke with other tongues, magnifying God. After this, Peter baptized them.

Before this time, Jews did not associate with Gentiles and certainly didn't go into their homes. This was the beginning of Gentiles receiving the message of the gospel, and it all came about because Peter saw a vision from God and obeyed the voice of the Holy Spirit.

A Vision After My Husband's Passing

Right after my husband passed, I had been praying, and the Holy Spirit brought certain scriptures to my mind. Then I saw in a vision a hammer hitting a bubble. After this I saw many small bubbles going out from that large bubble in every direction. I heard the Holy Spirit speak in my thoughts: "The devil thought that he had hit this ministry so big that it would paralyze it. But this thing is about to break out in all directions. People are going to rise up and take responsibility and ownership of the vision to expand it beyond where it is now. There will be a multiplication of the vision."

He said to me that He would raise up our family, our staff, and our congregation to go out and impact the world, and that the seeds Billy Joe had planted in all of us would be multiplied.

When I saw this vision and I heard the Holy Spirit speak into my heart, I knew I had to share this with others that God would enable us to move forward. I sensed a special grace come upon my life to lead them. I knew people were watching me and our family. I had to think not about what everyone's opinions might be. I had a strong impression from God that was moving me.

I didn't know that two weeks earlier when I was out of Billy Joe's hospital room for a few minutes, he had asked for a piece of paper to write a note. He wrote that he felt in his absence from the pulpit that I should step up and fill that place. Of course, the Board would need to vote on it.

The Board did meet and asked if I would step forward to be the Lead Pastor at that time. Since the Lord had already spoken to my heart, it was a confirmation to me that I had heard correctly. I knew I didn't have the same gifting as my husband, but I knew the voice of the Lord, and I heard Him say Zechariah 4:6: "This is the word of the LORD...Not by might, nor by power, but by my spirit, saith the LORD of hosts."

He spoke to me that He would raise up men and women around me who had the strength and giftings that I lacked. They would help give me insight and together we would move the ship forward. I remember reading 1 Chronicles 12:22, which says that God surrounded David with an army of mighty men and women who came to help, who understood what was needed and were prepared for the moment. I felt God speak to me that He was bringing mighty people around me to help me.

Many times I feel the enemy seeks to get our thoughts upon ourselves and what we lack, but if we can let God help us see beyond ourselves and believe, He can work in amazing ways.

I had to think not about the opinions of others. In the world we live in today, many like to voice their opinions (especially on social media) about everything. This is why we must hear from God and be led by Him and surround ourselves with other believers who are seeking to hear from God too.

Through the years Billy Joe had trained believers to do the work of the ministry. Instead of just looking to special men or women to do what Jesus has called us to do, in the last days believers will rise up and be used mightily in signs and wonders to demonstrate the gospel.

I believed that I heard the Holy Spirit say to me that I had to rise up and steady the ship and take it forward; that I was who people had seen by Billy Joe's side through the years, and they would look to see what I would do.

I knew immediately that I needed to step up to speak into the congregation so they would know Jesus would enable us to go forward. I shared the vision with our staff and congregation.

Even though my mind was somewhat fuzzy at times in those first four to six months, I sensed a bubble of grace surrounding and supporting us. As a congregation and staff, we healed together and stood together with the same calling and grace from God's Spirit as we moved forward, and we have expanded the vision over these past few years.

The Holy Spirit also spoke to me that I would be a transition pastor, and that my son Paul would rise to become the Lead Pastor. I knew that all of my children and their spouses would rise and be used by God to reach this generation, and that, along with others, I would continue to minister with them, bringing in the harvest, discipling those coming into God's Kingdom, and mentoring those called to ministry. I later found out that a week before he passed, Billy Joe had called our associate pastor to say that he felt Paul was the one to lead in the future but wasn't ready yet.

Seek Jesus

Let me say that I believe it is important not to seek dreams and visions, but to seek Jesus and be open to His speaking to us in whatever ways He desires. God wants us to learn how to hear His voice daily in His written Word and in a prayer relationship with Him.

Let's look at several ways that God speaks.

1. He speaks through His written Word, the Scriptures. (See Psalm 119:105, NKJV.)

2. He speaks in prayer as we ask Him to speak into our thoughts. (See Proverbs 16:3, AMP.)

3. He speaks through dreams and visions. (See Job 33:14–16; Acts 18:9–11; 22:17–21, NKJV.)

4. He speaks through others. (See Exodus 18:17–26, NKJV.)

5. He speaks through prophetic words that we receive from the Lord or that others may say. (See Acts 11:27–30; 21:9–13, NKJV; 1 Timothy 1:18, NKJV.)

6. He speaks through the witness of the Holy Spirit with our spirit by a knowing within. (See Acts 16:6–7; 20:23; Romans 8:16, NKJV.) Sometimes it is words that are said by someone else that witness with your spirit (possibly in conversation or in listening to a sermon being preached). It is when you have a strong knowing within about something, and you cannot shake it or dismiss it.

There is a draw of heaven to communicate with us while we live on this earth, because God wants to help us. This is why James 4:8 (NKJV) says, "Draw near to God and He will draw near to you...." He will speak to your heart with His thoughts.

Unusual Dreams

In January 2010 we were having a planning meeting for a special Night to Honor Israel—music, video, and a speaking production that we do to connect our Christian community with our Jewish community in our city. It had been two months since my husband's passing.

After the meeting, a Jewish man with whom my husband and I had become friends, came to speak to me. He was moved to tears as he shared with me something that had happened to his wife.

The year prior to this, he and his wife had come to us for prayer regarding his wife's illness. She had been diagnosed with a serious cancer. She was going to start medical treatment for it, but wanted my husband to pray for a miracle intervention from God. They didn't know that my husband had also been diagnosed with a serious illness, but at the time, it seemed to be improving. Billy Joe prayed for her, binding the spirit of infirmity and speaking to the cancer to leave her body in Jesus' name. We released our faith for a miracle.

She had begun a treatment right before my husband had to go into the hospital. Because of the aggressiveness of the cancer, she was scheduled to have more medical treatments. However, early Sunday morning of November 22, 2009, when my husband passed, his wife had a dream of my husband Billy Joe coming to her and telling her that her cancer was gone and she was healed.

That week when she returned to the doctor to be examined, the doctor was shocked and said that he didn't know what had happened but that she no longer had any sign of cancer in her body. Her husband was weeping as he told me the story.

Months later, this family was moving to Israel. Right before leaving, they felt they needed to come to say good-bye to our church, so they attended our first Sunday morning church service. It just happened to be Pentecost Sunday, and I shared a message about the day of Pentecost (also known as the Jewish Feast of Firstfruits). I explained that Jesus had told the disciples that they were to go to Jerusalem, to pray and wait for the promise of the Holy Spirit.

As I shared the connection from the Old Testament to the New Testament, focusing on Joel 2:28 and Acts, chapters 1 and 2, God had already been preparing their hearts. As I gave an invitation to come and receive prayer, the wife was the first person to come. Many others came as well, reaching from one side of the altar to the other.

After praying the salvation prayer and asking for the baptism of the Holy Spirit, I had a chance to speak with the wife. She experienced the presence of God in a very tangible way. She left weeping to go to the women's room, and when she returned they decided to stay for the second service as well.

At the end of the second service, the husband came forward for prayer, along with many others. Again, we prayed, and he had the same experience as his wife had. The Lord placed the right couple behind them to pray for them, because that couple had financially helped many Jews leave the former Soviet Union to move to Israel and had built soup kitchens around Israel to give humanitarian aid. God is so amazing in how He works supernaturally in lives!

My Dream

I only had one dream about my husband after he passed away. I had been pastoring our church for a few months, and I had been seeking God each day in the Word and in prayer.

I knew God wanted to continue using Victory as a place for healing, deliverance, and salvation just as my late husband, Billy Joe, had ministered when he was here on earth.

We were seeing people come from all walks of life and get saved; delivered from drugs, alcohol, and sexual bondages; healed; and connected in church with other believers. We also began to see people healed supernaturally of illnesses such as multiple sclerosis, cancer, HIV/AIDS virus, and healed of things doctors said they would have the rest of their lives.

Because my husband and I had a wonderful relationship, I have been able to talk about our lives together when he lived here on earth and refer to things he said or did in a healthy way. It always touches my heart when people tell me stories about how he ministered to their lives. I say this because I still have good memories that I can reflect upon at times. However, I don't dwell in the past where I don't relate to people now.

It was one night in February 2010 that I had a dream where I was standing in a line of people. Suddenly, I felt that my late husband was standing beside me. I turned, and there he was. I touched his arm and said, "Are you real?" He replied, "Yes." Then he indicated that he would come and go. I awakened from my dream and dismissed it from my thoughts. I knew my mind had to stay focused on God's Word. Sometimes people become focused on a dream or words someone else has spoken instead of focusing on God's Word, and they become vulnerable to deception. We have to guard our hearts but also realize that our loved ones are still very much alive in heaven and they are involved in various activities in heaven. They aren't just floating around on clouds.

An acquaintance recently shared a dream she had about her younger brother who had died suddenly from a brain aneurysm. He'd been a chef after returning from duty in Vietnam, and in her dream, she smelled baking bread before she saw him. She stepped into what appeared to be a bakery, where her brother was adding some finishing touches to copper-lined storage bins. Fresh breads and rolls would be displayed in the bins. Initially, she was shocked to see him looking so peaceful and happy. She said, "Oh, Bob, your hair has grown back already!" (His head had been shaved prior to surgery in an attempt to save his life.)

He smiled and said, "My hair is thicker than it's ever been." She then asked if this was his shop. He said it was and that it was something he'd always dreamed of. Suddenly, he said he needed to leave for a moment, but would return. She was awakened by her telephone at her bedside. The dream was over, but the calm reassurance that dream brought of her brother's happiness in heaven forever settled the grief she'd experienced.

Let me say that I firmly believe the Bible says that we are not to communicate with the dead. I do believe Hebrews 12:11 indicates that they are aware of us here on earth and desire that we finish our race with a determined endurance and victory. Sometimes people open themselves up to wrong spirits when they cannot let go of the loved one who has passed.

Isaiah 8:19–20 (MSG) says:

> When people tell you, "Try out the fortunetellers. Consult the spiritualists. Why not tap into the spirit-world, get in touch with the dead?" tell them, "No, we're going to study

the Scriptures." People who try the other ways get nowhere—
a dead end! Frustrated and famished, they try one thing after
another....

As Christians we have a promise that our loved ones who have
passed away who received Jesus while on earth, are with Jesus, and
they still have an interest in us here on the earth. In fact, Scripture
says they surround us.

> *Therefore, since we also have such a large cloud of witnesses*
> *surrounding us, let us lay aside every weight and the sin that*
> *so easily ensnares us. Let us run with endurance the race*
> *that lies before us, keeping our eyes on Jesus, the source and*
> *perfecter of our faith, who for the joy that lay before Him*
> *endured a cross and despised the shame and has sat down at*
> *the right hand of God's throne.*
>
> —HEBREWS 12:1–2, HCSB

According to Noah Webster's *1828 American Dictionary of the*
English Language, a "witness" is someone who knows and sees in
order to give testimony or evidence to something. The Greek word
for *witness* is *martus,* which means witness and more specifically, one
who is mindful; one who has seen and heard, but also someone who
has lived and proven the genuineness of their faith in Christ and some
who have undergone violent death for the sake of Christ. This scripture tells us they surround us here on earth. I believe they surround
us with prayer.

I believe our loved ones who have died and gone on to heaven are
praying for us. My husband prayed regularly for me and our children
while he lived on earth, and I believe he still prays for us.

I have had a few moments when I felt as if he were probably smiling. I have had other moments when I thought he was probably dancing for the Lord with joy along with me while I was singing and dancing for the Lord here. I know he is still alive, even though he is not physically with me.

Dwight L. Moody once said:

> Someday you will read in the paper that Dwight L. Moody of East Northfield is dead. Don't you believe a word of it. At that moment I shall be more alive than I am now. I shall have gone up higher, that is all. Out of this old clay tenement into a body that is immortal, a body that death cannot touch, that sin cannot taint, a body fashioned like unto His glorious body.[11]

Those who have gone on to heaven started something we are to finish. They are very interested in whether we reach the goal that is set before us. This is one more reason why we need to listen to the Holy Spirit's convictions and promptings and obey His voice.

Unexplainable Dreams and Visions

Audrey Poteet had been the pastor of a small church in Arkansas. (Audrey's relatives shared this story with me.) He has also had a prison ministry where he has ministered to hardened men who were not easy to convince with the gospel.

---

11 Wholesomewords.org. *Echoes from Glory,* Dwight L. Moody, American Evangelist.

When he first started going to minister in the prison, Audrey shared how he had a dream about Billy Joe. (He didn't know him personally.) This was a few weeks after Billy Joe died.

Audrey had been discouraged in ministry and didn't think much was happening through his life. He had a dream that Billy Joe came to him and said, "I'm Pastor Billy Joe, and I pastored a church in Tulsa that was a big ministry. I'm from Arkansas too," he said as we walked together talking.

Then he said, "What you are doing is just as important as what I've done." They spoke a little bit as they kept walking. Then he went on.

Audrey saw some other people and said, "I just spoke with Pastor Billy Joe." They said, "You couldn't have, because he died." He said, "Well, I did."

After that, he woke up. He felt renewed in his vision of the jail ministry. Later one day as he was ministering at the jail, the hardest of criminals began weeping and coming to the Lord. Sixteen hundred men came to the Lord right after that.

Other Stories—Nicaragua

In March 2014 I was ministering in a large soul-winning outreach in Nicaragua. We had never been to Nicaragua before. My late husband had not been there before either. Several youth and adults went to different sites in Nicaragua the same week. Our team was in Leon, Nicaragua. I taught a pastors' seminar during the day for two days and ministered in a women's conference the third day.

That weekend we had a large outdoor gathering where 60,000 came to listen to music and rap, preaching, and then prayer for healing among the people. God worked miracles among the people, and many received salvation that night. We gave out thousands of books, along with starting a Bible school.

The first day of the pastors' seminar, a Nicaraguan lady minister came up to me afterward and said she had seen a vision of someone behind me as I spoke. She said she rubbed her eyes because she thought she was imagining it, but yet, every time she opened her eyes, he was still there. We had given out books translated into Spanish that my late husband had written, titled "No Fear." She said when she saw the picture of the man on the back of the book, it looked like the man in the vision she had seen.

The next day I was speaking to pastors in a conference. A couple who pastored a church three hours away from Leon came to the pastors' meeting and afterward told one of our team members that they both had had a dream the night before. Both had dreamed about the same man who came to them in their dream, telling them to go to this church and they would get answers to their questions.

That morning the wife told her husband about her dream, and the husband said he had had the same dream. The husband could not go, but insisted that his wife go. She had to get directions to where the church was located. When she arrived she said the lady speaking in front was answering all of their questions. Then when the book was passed out to all who had attended the conference that day, she saw the picture of my late husband on the back of the book. She came to the front to ask my assistant, "Who is this man on the back of the book?" Then she said he was the man in her and her husband's dreams last night.

The third day, a young woman came to the women's meeting and was crying after most of the people had left. I asked through an interpreter what was wrong. She replied that she and her husband and two children were being evicted from their house. She had been worried about where they would go. That night before coming to the women's conference, she had a dream. In the dream, a white man had come to her and said to go to a certain church and she would get help.

The next day she went to the church where we were having the women's meeting. After I spoke, she received one of our little booklets, "You Are Valuable." When she turned it over, she started crying because the picture of the man on the back of the book was the same man who came to her in her dream.

She said, "I don't know this man. Why would he come to me in my dream?" I didn't have an explanation then. I didn't mention that he had passed away. I simply told her that obviously God wanted her to know she was valuable and that He was going to take care of her and her family. One of the ladies at the church then took her information to follow up in helping her.

That week of unusual happenings caused me to stop and think about Hebrews 12:1, which says, "Such a large crowd of witnesses is all around us!" (CEV). Other scriptures I remembered were Mark 9:1–10; Matthew 17:1–9; and Luke 9:28–30, which tell about Peter, James, and John going with Jesus to a high mountain apart from others. Suddenly Jesus was transfigured before them. Then they saw Moses and Elijah appear with Him, talking with Him. Jesus told them to wait to tell that incident after He was to rise from the dead.

I thought about that incident that Elijah, of course, had never died but had been caught up to heaven. In fact, he is to be one of the two witnesses to come during the Tribulation, along with Enoch who also never died but was caught up into heaven. Moses, however, had died on earth. Moses had been dead 1,500 years, confined in a paradise place called Abraham's bosom, with other righteous souls who had died waiting for the Messiah to raise them up (Luke 16:19-22).

When Jesus died and was raised from the dead, Scripture tells us that graves were opened and many bodies of the saints who slept arose and went into the city of Jerusalem. These were seen by many before ascending into heaven. (See Matthew 27:52-53.) This, of course, was a one-time event. They were on their way up to heaven to the home Jesus had prepared for them. (See John 14:1–4.)

I have not dwelt on these unusual happenings. I believe we are to keep our focus on Jesus. However, I believe that heaven and earth are drawing closer together and that God's heaven is definitely involved in what is happening here on earth.

Another Story of a Woman's Experience

I remember reading from Rebecca Springer's book, *My Dream of Heaven*. She wrote that when she was very ill at the point of death, she was away from loved ones who would normally help care for her. She wrote:

> I prayed that the dear Christ would help me to realize His blessed presence, and that since the beloved ones of earth could not minister to me, I might feel the influence of the other dear ones who are "all ministering spirits." Especially did I ask to be sustained should I indeed be called to pass through the dark waters alone. Christ's peace enfolded me.

A Vision Began

> After a day and night of intense suffering, I seemed to be
> standing on the floor by the bed . . . Someone was standing
> by me, and when I looked up, I saw my husband's favorite
> brother who 'crossed the flood' many years ago . . . "My
> dear brother Frank! How good of you to come!" Frank
> then said, "It was a great joy to me that I could do so, little
> sister. Shall we go now?" as he drew me beyond the room
> and to the window.[12]

In this dream, she was told by Frank, her brother-in-law, that she
would return back to the room later after going to heaven.

Rebecca lived from 1832 to 1904. She felt in writing this book it
would help Christians whose loved ones have passed away know that
heaven is real and beautiful, and that their loved ones are happy and
still very active in eternity.

In early April 2016, I was awakened at four in the morning to the
smell of electrical burning—a smell that was familiar from October
1991 when all of our family escaped as our house burned in the
middle of the night. (It was hard to breathe because of a burning
sensation that night of our fire.)

No alarm sounded. I just woke up to the smell. I'd stayed up late
the night before studying so I had been in a deep sleep. I rose from
my bed and walked through my house searching for the source of the
problem. I awakened my friend who lives upstairs, but the fumes were

---

12 Rebecca Springer. *My Dream of Heaven* (First ed. *Intra Muros),* White
Crow Productions, Ltd., 1898 (available on Amazon.com), 1–4.

definitely not coming from upstairs. She came downstairs to help me locate the problem.

When we turned on the lights, we saw a tan-colored smoke that saturated the lower level of my house from the ceiling to the floor. We opened the back door for air and to walk outside to see if there was any fire we could see, but found none. As I stepped close to the ceiling vents, I realized that they were the source of the smoke. There was also a grinding sound coming from the vents. I turned off my heating and air-conditioning system and then felt I should turn off the breaker to my furnace.

Two years earlier I'd had the entire heat and air system checked and was told it was old and wouldn't last long into the future. They also said I could wait awhile to get a new one. I asked what would be the first thing to go out when it died, and they said it would be the furnace.

The weather had changed and become much cooler on that night in April, and I had turned on the furnace before going to bed. I had a thought that the smoke was carbon monoxide poisoning and that something supernatural had awakened me. I knew heaven was watching over us.

I went back to my bed and heard that same small voice speak strongly inside me to open the windows near me to breathe fresh air, and I slept a little longer. I was to speak the next morning at our school chapel meeting. After chapel I returned to my office just as the phone rang. It was one of our pastoral staff. She was crying as she spoke, telling me that she was awakened about 4:30 a.m. from a dream. She shared that in her dream Pastor Billy Joe had appeared to her asking, "Would you pray for my family?" She arose and began writing down the names of all of our family—children and grandchildren—and prayed for God's help, His protection, and His intervention in our lives.

She had no knowledge that I had just experienced the smoke in my home early that morning. I thanked her for her very timely prayers and hung up to call for service to the heat and air-conditioning system. Sure enough, the heating unit had died and the motor had kept running, which made the grinding sound. When I described the smoke that had filled the house in the lower level, the technician agreed that it was carbon monoxide poisoning. God had delivered our lives!

We have had prayer day and night at our church for many, many years, beginning with early morning prayer, that I often lead along with other prayer leaders. A few years ago, my ministry position changed, and God raised up another woman to oversee the prayer ministry. Later, I heard the Holy Spirit telling me to again lead one of the daily prayer times. A while later, the Lord directed my heart to continue leading in that prayer time, specifically for the supernatural help and intervention of heaven for our church and all of its various branches of ministry, our church family, staff, our nation, state, and city, and the harvest God desires to reach.

We have witnessed God's divine intervention at various times. I say this to stress how strongly I believe it is critically important to be open to hear God's voice daily and obey His voice in what may seem to be a small thing to you and me at the moment, but in the spiritual world, our obedience could literally save lives. "Today, if you hear his voice, do not harden your hearts..." (Hebrews 3:7, NIV).

If you think you hear God's voice, I urge you not to shove the thought aside.

The spiritual realm around us is very real. I believe the closer we get to the end of the age, the closer heaven and earth are. I also believe there is more activity happening between the two than ever before.

In the book *Heaven* by Randy Alcorn, he writes:

> The people of God in Heaven have a strong familial connection with those on earth who are called their "fellow servants and brothers" (Revelation 6:11). We share the same Father "from whom every family in heaven and on earth is named." ...
>
> There is not a wall of separation within the bride of Christ. We are one family with those who've gone to Heaven ahead of us. After we go to Heaven, we'll still be one family with those yet on Earth. These verses demonstrate a vital connection between the events and people in Heaven and the events and people on Earth.[13]

Randy Alcorn goes on to say that those in heaven who have been martyred remember their lives on earth. They ask God to intervene on earth and act on their behalf. "How long... until You judge the inhabitants of the Earth and avenge our blood?"[14] They ask for judgment on their persecutors who are still at work hurting others. They are acting in solidarity with and in effect interceding for the suffering saints on earth. This suggests that saints in heaven are both seeing and praying for the saints on earth (Revelation 6:10).

If the martyrs in heaven know that God hasn't yet brought judgment on their persecutors, it seems evident that the inhabitants of the

---

13 Randy Alcorn. *Heaven,* Tyndale House Publishers, Inc., 2004 by Eternal Perspective Ministries, 67.

14 Ibid., 66.

present heaven can see what's happening on earth, at least to some extent. When Babylon is brought down, an angel points to events happening on earth and says, "Rejoice over her, thou heaven, and ye holy apostles and prophets; for God hath avenged you on her" (Revelation 18:20).

If saints are going to return with Christ to set up His millennial kingdom (Revelation 19:11–14), it seems unthinkable to imagine they would have remained ignorant of the culmination of human history taking place on earth... Those on earth may be ignorant of heaven, but those in heaven are *not* ignorant of earth.[15]

---

15 Ibid., 69.

Chapter 12

GOD'S PROMISES FOR WIDOWS

GOD HAS PROMISED THAT He will support widows who have given their lives to Him and who believe in His Word and supernatural help. If you are a widow, take time to write out these scriptures and meditate on them:

Psalm 146:9, NLT—

> *"The LORD . . . cares for the orphans and widows. . . ."*

Psalm 146:9, MSG—

> *"God . . . takes the side of orphans and widows. . . ." God is on your side. He'll deal with other people on your behalf.*

Psalm 146:9, NCV—

> *"He defends the orphans and widows . . ." God will act as our lawyer and defend us. God has a way of speaking to people who attempt to do wrong to the widow.*

Psalm 146:9, CEV—

> *"He defends the rights of orphans and widows. . . ."*

Proverbs 15:25, NLT—

"*The Lord…protects the property of widows.*"

Proverbs 15:25, ERV—

"*The Lord…protects a widow's property.*"

Psalm 68:5, AMP—

"*A father of the fatherless and a judge and protector of the widows is God in His holy habitation.*"

Psalm 68:5, NLT—

"*Father to the fatherless, defender of widows—this is God, whose dwelling is holy.*"

Psalm 68:5, MEV—

"*A father to the fatherless, and a protector of the widows, is God in His holy habitation.*"

I believe these scriptures for my life and for my children:

Psalm 68:5, NET—

"*He is a father to the fatherless and an advocate for widows. God rules from his holy palace.*"

Psalm 68:5, GNT—

"*God, who lives in his sacred Temple, cares for orphans and protects widows.*"

For all who may have experienced a loved one passing into eternity, when we stay connected with the church and continue seeking the Lord, He gives us the supply of His Spirit in our lives.

He strengthens us each day in going forward. He connects us with relationships that can help us. He is able to protect us from vulnerability to wrong choices. So we see it's not only spending time individually with the Lord, but it's also spending time with other Christians who sharpen us spiritually that enables us to go forward. It's in giving out of ourselves as well. We find a place where we are needed and can serve, and this keeps us from becoming self-focused or drawing away into depression.

Testimony of Dealing with Wife's Death

Psalm 68:6 (NIV) tells us that "God sets the lonely in families." When we walk through a time where a loved one passes, God Himself comforts us in our time of need when we draw to Him. However, He also brings comfort by placing relationships around us that strengthen us. This can happen through being a part of a life-giving church. Through these God-given relationships, He restores us and shows us that His hand of purpose is still upon our lives.

A man in our church experienced this:

About two or three months after his wife went to heaven, the Lord impressed on his heart to start greeting people at the door again in church services.

Our church host team had been such a blessing to him, and he always considered it a privilege to serve.

At one particular service, the man sat behind a young couple, who were the parents of a preschool-aged son. The man and his wife were expecting their second child.

To make a long story short, the couple turned out to be a wonderful blessing to the man. They became close friends and invited him to be part of their family. They began to save him a seat every week at church, and sometimes in the services, they asked him to hold their baby daughter, who often fell asleep in his lap.

What joy their actions brought to the widower, especially since he and his wife had no children of their own. This was an answer to prayer and a testimony of God's goodness. Along with his connect group and visits from church members and their prayers, his life has moved forward from "strength to strength" according to Psalm 84:4–7, MEV—"Blessed are those who dwell in Your house; they continually praise You. Selah. Blessed is the man whose strength is in You, in whose heart are the paths to Zion. As they pass through the Valley of Baca [weeping], they make it a spring…they go from strength to strength…."

Psalm 84:4, 7, AMP—

"Blessed (happy, fortunate, to be envied) are those who dwell in Your house and Your presence; they will be singing Your praises… They go from strength to strength [increasing in victorious power]…."

In this scripture, the "Valley of Baca" was the Valley of Weeping. Instead of it drowning the person in grief, the psalmist states the person allowed the Lord to take them from "strength to strength."

There is strength when we are strong with God's house (His sanctuary of worship).

Other Scriptures to Meditate

2 Corinthians 1:3–4, NLT—

"God is our merciful Father and the source of all comfort. He comforts us in all our troubles so that we can comfort others. When they are troubled, we will be able to give them the same comfort God has given us."

2 Corinthians 1:3, NKJV—

"Blessed be the God and Father of our Lord Jesus Christ, the Father of mercies and God of all comfort."

Isaiah 61:2, NIV—

"[The Lord was sent to] comfort all who mourn."

Isaiah 61:2–3, GNT—

"He has sent me to proclaim that the time has come when the Lord will save his people–to give to those who mourn . . . joy and gladness instead of grief, a song of praise instead of sorrow. . . ."

When we seek the Lord, He comforts our souls and ministers peace to our spirits. He enables us to praise and worship, and then He enables us to have strength and grace to do whatever He says to do.

Psalm 84:5, MSG—

"Blessed are all those in whom you live, whose lives become roads you travel...."

2 Corinthians 12:9, MEV—

"He said to me, 'My grace is sufficient for you, for My strength is made perfect in weakness!...'"

2 Corinthians 12:9, GNT—

"My grace is all you need, for my power is greatest when you are weak...."

Here we see a different side of grace. God's grace is His divine empowerment, enabling us to do what we could not do in our natural strength or ability.

Psalm 23:4—

"[His] rod (Word) *and* [His] *staff* (Holy Spirit) *they comfort me."* They support me, encourage me, guide me, protect me, give me correction when I need it, and reveal things to me that I would not know otherwise.

Philippians 4:19, CEV—

"I pray that God will take care of all your needs with the wonderful blessings that come from Christ Jesus!"

2 Corinthians 1:20—

"For all the promises of God in him (in Christ Jesus) *are yea, and in him Amen...."*

Psalm 5:12—

The Lord surrounds me like a shield with His favor.

Psalm 91:4—

He is my shield and buckler to protect me.

Psalm 46:1–2, MEV—

"God is our refuge and strength, a well-proven help in trouble. Therefore we will not fear. . . ."

Psalm 34:7, NLT—

"For the angel of the Lord is a guard; he surrounds and defends all who fear him."

Psalm 34:17-18, NLT—

"The Lord hears his people when they call to him for help. He rescues them from all their troubles. The Lord is close to the brokenhearted; he rescues those whose spirits are crushed."

Psalm 27:1, NLT—

"The Lord is my light and my salvation—so why should I be afraid? The Lord is my fortress, protecting me from danger, so why should I tremble?"

Philippians 1:6, NKJV—

"Being confident of this very thing, that He who has begun a good work in you will complete it until the day of Jesus Christ."

Jeremiah 29:11, NLT—

"'For I know the plans I have for you,' says the Lord. 'They are plans for good and not for disaster, to give you a future and a hope.'"

Hebrews 13:5, NLT—

"[The Lord has said], 'I will never fail you (leave you), I will never abandon you.'"

Proverbs 3:5–6, NKJV—

"Trust in the Lord with all your heart, and lean not on your own understanding; in all your ways acknowledge Him, and He shall direct your paths."

Isaiah 40:29, 31, MEV—

"He gives power to the faint, and to those who have no might He increases strength . . . But those who wait upon the Lord shall renew their strength; they shall mount up with wings as eagles, they shall run and not be weary, and they shall walk and not faint."

Isaiah 40:31, AMP—

"But those who wait for the Lord [who expect, look for, and hope in Him] shall change and renew their strength and power; they shall lift their wings and mount up [close to God] as eagles [mount up to the sun]; they shall run and not be weary, they shall walk and not faint or become tired."

Psalm 27:14—

"Wait on the Lord: be of good courage, and he shall strengthen thine heart: wait, I say, on the Lord."

Part 3

HEAVEN—OUR FINAL HOME

Chapter 13

HEAVEN

In the beginning God created the heavens and the earth.
—Genesis 1:1, NLT

H EAVEN IS MENTIONED 582 times in the Bible—327 times in the Old Testament and 255 times in the New Testament.

When the topic of heaven is brought up in conversation, most people believe in heaven, but they know little about it. Most people think of a place far away in space somewhere, where God lives and people go there after they die. Beyond that, people are hesitant to say what they believe when it comes to the subject. Movies and television are also an influencing factor since our society seems to be media driven.

Some people have the idea that people in heaven walk around on clouds while angels play harps. In fact, some have spoken misconceptions about angels that when some have died that they become angels. No! This is wrong. Scripture indicates that God created angels different than people. People are created in the image of God—spirit, soul, and body (Genesis 1:26). We were created with the capacity to receive the Spirit of Jesus into our hearts.

Angels are spirit beings, but they cannot be born again. God's angels are simply spirit beings who love and serve God because they understand He created them. They understand His purposes, His goodness, and His justice.

Even though most people don't know a lot about heaven, there is a feeling that it is a good place, and it is where they want to go when they die.

There are a lot of misconceptions and beliefs about heaven and who will go there. Some people don't believe in heaven or hell. They believe these words are figures of speech. Some people might say, "That was hell on earth," or "That experience was heaven on earth." But whether or not a person believes in heaven and hell, they are real places, and every person on earth will end up one day in one place or the other.

Some people believe that everyone will go to heaven whether or not they accept Jesus Christ as their Lord and Savior while on earth. They say there are many roads to heaven and that Jesus is just one of many. (This is the belief of the Inclusion Gospel or Universalism.) However, Jesus made it clear in John 14:1-6 where He told His disciples that He was going to leave them and go prepare a place for them in His Father's dwelling place (heaven). He said He would come again and receive them to Himself so they could be with Him.

Then Jesus gave the clear direction saying, "I am the way, the truth, and the life. No one can come to the Father (God) except through Me" (John 14:6, NKJV). This means that in order to go to heaven, we must first accept Jesus Christ as Lord and Savior or the only way to heaven. Why? Because Jesus is the only Son that God has.

In John 3:16–21, Jesus told us that God loved the world so much that He gave His only Son Jesus to come to earth, die on the cross to take our sins, deliver us from Satan's domain, and then be raised from the dead to raise us from spiritual death to spiritual life.

What we do with Jesus is the deciding factor on whether or not we go to heaven.

In an article that Dr. Charles Trombley wrote in his newsletter in 2002, he said:

> Satan's end-time scheme will be to unite all religions under one banner—Jesus. Not the real Jesus, but another Jesus. There will be a push to convince people that we all worship the same God, but He has different names.
>
> Satan can't succeed by totally rejecting the historical Jesus, so he'll redefine Him. For example, Muslims believe in Jesus as only one of many prophets and that Mohammed is the greatest prophet. They do not believe He is the Son of God. To them, that is blasphemy.
>
> Buddhists believe Jesus is goodness resident in all men. Hindus believe in Jesus as one of their millions of gods. Unitarians believe in Jesus, but only as a morally upright human. Jehovah's Witnesses believe Jesus is actually Michael the archangel. Christian Scientists believe Jesus is perfect thought. Mormons believe Jesus is one of a council of gods. New Agers believe Jesus will be what anyone wants to make Him since all men are potential gods.
>
> Secularists, liberals, cultists, and unbelievers agree that Jesus was a compassionate, gracious, and truly good man. His morals and teaching were unexcelled, but He was not God in His Son redeeming the world unto Himself. They see Jesus as just one of many ways to God. However, Jesus

made it clear that He was the only way to God the Father, the Creator of heaven and earth and every living thing.

Second Corinthians 5:19 (NKJV) says, "God was in Christ reconciling the world to Himself...." Jesus said, "He who has seen Me has seen the Father..." (John 14:9, NKJV). Jesus declared who He is over and over. He said in Revelation 1:8 (NKJV), "I am the Alpha and the Omega, the Beginning and the End...who is and who was and who is to come, the Almighty."

First John 5:11–12 tells us, "God has given us eternal life and this life is in His Son. He who has the Son has life; he who does not have the Son of God does not have life." Eternal life is not a sensual paradise with seventy virgins for a man's pleasure as some believe.

Jesus said, "This is eternal life, that they may know You, the only true God, and Jesus Christ whom You have sent" (John 17:3, NKJV).

Some have not wanted to believe in an afterlife, because they must think about where they stand in relationship with God and deep within they know they must repent and believe in Him. Scripture not only tells us about the afterlife, but many today have had documented medical reports of "out of body" experiences. These have come back to tell that heaven and hell are real places.

Kenneth E. Hagin shared the account where he as a young man was ill and suddenly, lying in bed, his heart stopped and he realized he was leaving his body. He could see his grandmother sitting beside him praying. Kenneth Hagin was a member of the local church.

When he was lifted out of his body, he began to descend into the lower parts of the earth to hell. But as he would get to the bottom of a pit, something pulled him back up and away from the horrible creature that had grabbed him. Three times he cried out, "God, I belong to the church. I've been baptized in water." No response came as he descended down to that horrible pit. Then a voice shook the place and the creature let go of his arm again. Some kind of magnetic force pulled him up again and back into his body that was lying on the bed in his house. His grandmother was still there praying.

That experience so impacted his life, he was never the same again. He became a committed Christian and was called into the ministry.

Jesus spoke of both heaven and hell when He walked on earth. He told us in John 11:25–26 (NKJV):

> I am the resurrection and the life. He who believes in Me, though he may die, he shall live. And whoever lives and believes in Me shall never die.

Life does not end at physical death. We just change locations of where we live. Those who have given their lives to Jesus step into eternity and move to heaven.

So what does the Bible say about heaven? First of all, Genesis 1:1 (NKJV) says that "God created the heavens...." Notice that the word "heavens" is plural. The Hebrew word here is *shamayim,* which indicates not only the sky above which we see, but also that which is higher that we cannot see. The Bible tells us that there are three heavens.

The Apostle Paul wrote:

> It is doubtless not profitable for me to boast. I will come to visions and revelations of the Lord:
> I know a man in Christ who fourteen years ago—whether in the body I do not know, or whether out of the body I do

*not know, God knows—such a one was caught up to the third
heaven.*

*And I know such a man—whether in the body or out of
the body I do not know, God knows—*

*How he was caught up into Paradise and heard inexpress-
ible words, which it is not lawful for a man to utter.*

—2 CORINTHIANS 12:1–4 (NKJV)

In these verses, Paul wrote that he had had a vision from God where
he was caught up to the third heaven, which he called "Paradise." He
wasn't sure if he had left his body or not. He said it was such an overwhelming experience that he could not speak about what he saw or
heard while he was there.

Today we have the documented accounts of people who told about
their life and death experiences. Many of these experiences happened
after an accident, a serious illness, or while having surgery.

Some have had the experience of seeing heaven. Others have
seen hell and come back to tell their experiences. The prophet Isaiah
was in prayer one day and experienced a vision of heaven. He was
distraught over the death of the king. He knew that whenever a king
died, the country immediately became vulnerable to enemies. Isaiah
was praying for the nation. As he prayed, he had a vision of heaven.

Isaiah 6:1–3 (NKJV) tells us, "In the year that King Uzziah died, I
saw the Lord sitting on a throne, high and lifted up, and the train of
His robe filled the temple. Above it stood seraphim…And one cried
to another and said, 'Holy, Holy, Holy is the Lord of hosts; the whole
earth is full of His glory.'"

Uzziah had become king at the age of 16 and ruled for 52 years. As
long as he sought the Lord, God made him prosper. He successfully

defended Judah against the belligerent Ammonites, Philistines, and Arabians, developed a long-standing army, and rebuilt the nation's fortifications, but he disobeyed God and became proud. He contracted leprosy and later died.

Isaiah had been an advisor to him in his court. Isaiah was also a cousin to King Uzziah. King Uzziah's son was selected to take his place. Isaiah was aware of the instability of the nation at the time of the king's death. He was seeking God about the nation. In a vision of heaven he saw God seated on His throne. This vision inspired Isaiah that God was still reigning over the people, and he heard the Lord say, "Who will I send to speak to the people?" Isaiah first recognized his own human weakness before God, saying, "Lord, I am a man of unclean lips." Then after an angel touched him, he said, "Here am I! Send me" (Isaiah 6:8, NKJV).

This story is powerful! How do you see the Lord? Sometimes after we have had a loved one pass away, we can only see ourselves. But when we seek God, He will reveal Himself still reigning in our lives.

Isaiah's vision of heaven came as he was seeking God in prayer and meditation. Heaven will always reveal that the Lord God Almighty reigns!

Chapter 14

THE FIRST HEAVEN

L ET'S TALK ABOUT HEAVEN. Second Corinthians 12:1–2 (NKJV) states:

> It is doubtless not profitable for me to boast. I will come to visions and revelations of the Lord.
> I know a man in Christ who fourteen years ago—whether in the body I do not know, or whether out of the body I do not know, God knows—such a one was caught up to the third heaven.

Scripture indicates there are three different heavens:

1. The sky above us and outer space;

2. A spiritual heaven; and

3. The heaven where God dwells.

Looking at the Old and New Testaments, we can see descriptions of these three heavens.

The first heaven is the heaven we see. This is the sky above us where there are clouds; where we see the sun, moon, and stars; where we see the birds fly and airplanes flying over us. It includes space beyond earth where rockets have gone to the moon and back as we have watched through technology. This first heaven is evident to the natural eye.

> *O Sovereign Lord! You made the heavens and earth by your strong hand and powerful arm. Nothing is too hard for you!*
> —JEREMIAH 32:17 (NLT)

> *"I handcrafted the skies and direct all the constellations in their turnings."*
> —ISAIAH 45:12 (MSG)

> *You* [Lord] *stretch out the starry curtain of the heavens.*
> —PSALM 104:2 (NLT)

> *You* [Lord] *made the moon to mark the seasons, and the sun knows when to set.*
> —PSALM 104:19 (NLT)

It is good to stop and think about the amazing beauty and detail of God's creation—how He thought about everything that surrounds us while living here on earth. It is good to be grateful and thankful to Him. The psalmist regularly thought about it, and he wrote, "Let all creation praise Him."

> *Let everything that has breath praise the* LORD.
> —PSALM 150:6 (NIV)

> *Praise the* LORD *from the heavens. Praise him in the heights above. Praise him, all his angels. Praise him, his entire heavenly army. Praise him, sun and moon. Praise him, all shining stars. Praise him, you highest heaven and the water above the*

sky. Let them praise the name of the LORD because they were created by his command.

—PSALM 148:1–5 (GW)

Throughout earth's history, God has given signs in the heavens that can be seen above us. After the flood that destroyed every living thing on earth, except Noah, his family, and the animals in the ark, God placed a rainbow in the sky as a sign of His covenant promise that there would never be another worldwide flood (Genesis 9:11–17).

In Exodus 10:21–23 we read that because of Pharaoh's oppression and hard heart toward the children of Israel, God caused darkness over the land of Egypt for three days, while at the same time there was light in the land where the children of Israel lived as a sign to Pharaoh that He (the God of Abraham, Isaac, and Jacob) was greater than Pharaoh or the gods that he worshipped.

In Joshua 10, five kings rose up together to fight against Joshua and the children of Israel. God told Joshua not to be afraid, that He would fight on their side. God sent a great hailstorm against the enemies and angelic help. Then Joshua spoke to the sun and moon to stand still for them to have daylight in conquering the enemies.

Dake's Reference Bible states that Greece, Egypt, China, and Mexico have historical records of a long day corresponding to the time of Joshua, that by counting the equinoxes, eclipses, and transits backward from our day to that of Joshua and counting them from the prime date of creation on Joshua's time, a whole day is missing and that by no possible mathematics can such a conclusion be avoided.[16]

---

16 Dake, Op. Cit., 265.

In 2 Kings 20:8, Hezekiah had been sick and near death. He asked for more time before dying so he could have a son to rise up in his place after he was gone. The Prophet Isaiah said God had heard his prayer, he would be healed, and he would be given 15 more years to live. Hezekiah asked what would be the sign that he would know he was healed. Isaiah said that the shadow of the sundial (their way of knowing time) would go backward ten degrees, and it did as Isaiah had spoken. Again, we see a sign in the heaven above us that affected time for generations to come.

Matthew 2:1–2 tells us that wise men came from the East to Israel following a certain star that had been predicted, indicating that a king would be born who was to rule the world. One prediction came in Numbers 24:17 that states that the Prophet Balaam went into a trance by the Spirit of God and began to prophesy of the future: "I see Him, but not now; I behold Him, but not near; a Star shall come out of Jacob; a Scepter shall rise out of Israel . . . and destroy all the sons of tumult" (NKJV).

The star of Bethlehem appeared when Jesus Christ was born—a sign in the heavens. Then Luke 2:9–14 tells that angels appeared in the sky over the shepherds watching their flocks at night outside of Bethlehem. The angel told them that Jesus (the Messiah) was born and that they would find Him in a manger in Bethlehem. (Note: The star of Bethlehem did not appear since that time until June 30, 2015.)

Many people today agree that this star appearing again after 2,000 years and the signs of the four blood moons correlating with the Jewish feasts of Passover and the feast of Tabernacles during 2014 and 2015 are signs indicating something is about to happen—something regarding end-time events being fulfilled that have been prophesied in the Scriptures.

Joel 2:30 and Acts 2:16–21 speak of how in the last days God will "shew wonders in the heaven above and signs in the earth…The sun shall be turned into darkness, and the moon into blood, before the coming of the great and awesome day of the Lord" (vv. 19–20, NKJV).

We are told to pay attention and be watchful, especially as we see signs happening around us regarding the times and seasons we are in.

God still uses signs in the heavens to give guidance or confirmation of His will at times. My late husband and I have seen signs in the skies through the years that gave us confirmation in God's leadings. When we sought God in the beginning of our church, a huge rainstorm came the first night as we prayed for God to pour out His Holy Spirit upon all who would come to Victory Christian Center. Later, when we were going to purchase the property to build the church, a rainstorm came one night and a huge bolt of lightning like a large finger came down upon the property. Someone happened to take a photo of it, and we made copies to give to the entire congregation.

Then after we had built our sanctuary, at the dedication weekend after it rained, a double rainbow appeared over our property, which was a sign to us of God's favor.

Evangelist Marilyn Hickey shared a story with us of her outreach to a South American city. Witches had prayed against her meeting. She and others prayed as God saved many people and worked miracles of healing among them. There was a double rainbow in the sky that lasted all three days where she held her meeting. The newspapers printed it as a sign from heaven over that part of the city.

Psalm 19:1–6 (NLT) says:

> *The heavens proclaim the glory of God. The skies display his craftsmanship. Day after day they continue to speak; night after night they make him known. They speak without a sound or word; their voice is never heard. Yet their message has gone throughout the earth and their words to all the world.*
>
> *God has made a home in the heavens for the sun. It bursts forth like a radiant bridegroom after his wedding. It rejoices like a great athlete eager to run the race. The sun rises at one end of the heavens and follows its course to the other end.*

Chapter 15

THE SECOND HEAVEN

Genesis 1:1 (MSG) says, "First this: God created the Heavens and Earth—all you see, all you don't see." There are two other heavens beyond the first heaven that are above us. These two heavens are unseen to the natural eye.

The second heaven that cannot be seen with the natural eye is the realm where angelic spirits from God and demonic spirits from Satan operate. This heavenly realm affects our natural realm on earth.

First, let's look at how God operates through His angelic spirits here on earth. Psalm 104:4 (NKJV) tells us that the Lord "makes His angels spirits, His ministers a flame of fire." Hebrews 1:14 (ERV) says, "All the angels are spirits who serve God and are sent to help those who will receive salvation."

Exodus 23:20–21 (NKJV) says:

> *"Behold, I send an Angel before you to keep you in the way and to bring you into the place which I have prepared. Beware of Him and obey His voice; do not provoke Him…for My name is in Him."*

In Exodus 14:19 God sent an angel to go before and behind Israel as they journeyed. The angel kept Pharaoh from catching up with them. Then as they arrived at the Red Sea, God told Moses to lift up his rod before the sea, and God caused the waters to part as the people of Israel walked across on dry ground. Then as Pharaoh and his army came behind them in the middle of the path where the sea had been, Moses lifted up his rod again and the waters came crashing down upon Pharaoh and his army and drowned them all.

It was messenger angels who came to Abraham in Genesis 18 to tell him Sarah would be having a baby soon, and they also told him about the soon judgment of Sodom and Gomorrah for which Abraham prayed.

An account is told in 2 Kings 6:8–23 (NIV) how Syria had been at war against Israel, wanting to wipe them out (even as it is today). Every time Syria plotted against Israel, it seemed that Israel would know ahead of time. The Syrian king asked who among them was the traitor, leaking information to Israel. One of the men said, "None of us, my lord the king… but Elisha, the prophet who is in Israel, tells the king of Israel the very words you speak in your bedroom" (v. 12, NIV).

The Syrian king decided to kill the prophet, so he took his troops and surrounded the city. Elisha's servant was afraid when he saw the multitude of military on horses surrounding them, and Elisha said, "Those who are with us are more than those who are with them" (v. 16, NIV). Then he prayed, "Open his eyes, Lord, so that he may see" (v. 17, NIV). The servant saw a mountain full of horses and chariots of fire around Elisha—the angelic host of heaven.

Think about it. If only one-third of the angels fell from heaven when Satan fell, then two-thirds have still been serving God. God's angelic spirits are in the majority over the demonic spirits. Elisha and Israel were delivered that day.

God's angels are powerful. We are told in 2 Chronicles 32:21 that Hezekiah and the Jewish people were being threatened by the king of Assyria and his mighty army. Syria's king had mocked Israel saying that God could not deliver them from his hand and that no one was greater than he. He tried to frighten the children of Israel.

Hezekiah and Isaiah the prophet prayed earnestly to God. God spoke to them that He was going to send a blast against the Syrian king so that he would return to his country and he would die. That night one angel came and destroyed 185,000 Syrian soldiers and the king, totally defeated, returned in shame to his homeland. He was then killed by his own sons.

Acts 12:1–17 tells us that there was great persecution of the early Christians. James had been killed and King Herod had thrown Peter in prison, planning to kill him also. But a group of Christians had started praying around the clock for Peter to be delivered. Because of prayer, the angel of the Lord came to Peter and awakened him to get up and follow him. The angel led him out of the prison and out of the city gate, and then disappeared. Peter then went to a house where believers were praying and told them about his supernatural deliverance.

Angelic spirits and demonic spirits can reveal themselves at times. Most of the time they are not seen with the natural eye, but they are actively operating around our lives.

I remember one time years ago when my two sons were babies. They were thirteen months apart in age, so I had them in a double stroller.

I was to get on an elevator on an occasion, and as I did, a man who seemed as if he was on some drug that made him wild looking jumped on with me. The door would not close. He frantically pushed all the buttons, but nothing happened.

I had prayed Psalm 91 that morning. I was very uneasy at this point. He jumped off and ran down a hall. The moment he left, the door closed.

Later, a man who had been watching said, "I saw that man jump on with you and your babies, and I prayed for God to send an angel to stop that man from harming you."

I believe an angel stood in the doorway and held the door open until the man got off. I didn't see the angel, but I know he was there.

Scripture lets us know that there is a spiritual realm so that we will be aware to cooperate with God and stop the enemy, Satan, from his plans and schemes. Obviously, earnest prayer brought angelic intervention that stopped the plan of the enemy in my life and in the account of Peter in Acts 12.

God has sent His angels on various assignments as He has looked for those whose hearts are pressing after Him. Hebrews 1:14 (LEB) says, "Are they not all spirits engaged in special service, sent on assignment for the sake of those who are going to inherit salvation?"

In Luke 1:26 the angel Gabriel came to Mary to tell her that she had been chosen as the virgin to fulfill Scripture in bringing God's Son into the world. An angel also appeared to Joseph telling him to take Mary as his wife.

After Jesus was born, the angel came to Joseph warning him to leave Bethlehem with the child and Mary and go to Egypt. Later, the angel returned to tell Joseph to leave Egypt and return to the land of Israel.

Throughout Scripture there are many accounts of God sending angels to come to the aid or give messages to God's people.

The important thing for us to know is that God's angels are moving between earth and heaven continually, responding to those who are pressing after God and believing for heaven's intervention.

In Genesis 28:12 (NKJV), Jacob dreamed a dream and "behold, a ladder was set up on the earth, and its top reached to heaven; and there the angels of God were ascending and descending on it."

Psalm 103:20 (ESV) says, "Bless the Lord, O you his angels, you mighty ones who do his word, obeying the voice of his word!"

When we speak God's Word with faith in prayer, His angels begin to move in performing that Word here on earth. They simply need us to voice what God has already spoken and to believe that God is faithful to do what He has said.

Spirits at War in the Heavenly Realm

Just as there are God's angelic spirits, there are evil spirits of Satan who are assigned to carry out his will. These are fallen angels who rebelled along with Satan and were cast out of heaven with him when he fell. These spirits seek to steal, kill, and destroy. They influence people to do evil. They seek to hinder those who are seeking God.

Job 1:6 says Satan and spirits had come before the Lord, along with the sons of God. The Lord asked Satan, "From where do you come?"

Satan replied that he had been "going to and fro on the earth, and from walking back and forth on it" (v. 7, NKJV).

First Peter 5:8 tells us a similar thing, that Satan walks about seeking whom he may devour, so we should be aware and watchful for his tactics.

Ephesians 6:12–13 (NLT) tells us:

> *For we are not fighting against flesh-and-blood enemies, but against evil rulers and authorities of the unseen world, against mighty powers in this dark world, and against evil spirits in the heavenly places. Therefore, put on every piece of God's armor so you will be able to resist the enemy in the time of evil. Then after the battle you will be standing firm.*

Paul describes the armor and says to put on the belt of truth (be truthful and be a person who loves the truth of God's Word), the breastplate of righteousness, having shoes on your feet of the preparation of the gospel of peace, taking the shield of faith, the helmet of salvation, and the sword of the Spirit, which is the Word of God, and praying always with all kinds of prayer in the Spirit.

Ephesians 6:12 tells us that just as there are different levels of soldiers in a military, there are different levels of demonic spirits in Satan's army. For example, certain spirits tend to hover over geographical regions while others try to oppress individuals with sickness, torment, addictive behavior, etc. Other demonic spirits seek to influence individuals in their thought life with deception, strife and division, fear, depression, or influencing someone to do evil, to hurt themselves, or to hurt others; to steal, kill, or destroy.

Daniel 10 gives us insight into the spiritual unseen battle that is going on between God's angelic spirits and Satan's demonic spirits.

Daniel had been taken captive with other Jews to the land of Babylon. (The location of Babylon today would be the land of Iraq.) Daniel had been praying, and he received a message from the angel Gabriel about the last days. Daniel made a decision to fast and pray in order to get understanding of this word from the Lord. Twenty-one days had passed as he was praying and asking God for the answer.

We read in Daniel 10:7–21 (NIV) that Daniel saw what appeared to be a man in a vision and heard the angel say:

> Do not be afraid... Since the first day that you set your mind to gain understanding and to humble yourself before your God, your words were heard, and I have come in response to them. But the prince of the Persian kingdom (a demonic spirit over the area where Daniel was living) resisted me twenty-one days. Then Michael, one of the chief princes (of God), came to help me, because I was detained there with the king of Persia. Now I have come to explain to you what will happen to your people in the future, for the vision concerns a time yet to come.
>
> —DANIEL 10:12–14 (NIV)

Then the angel told Daniel after he delivered the message to him that he would return to where he had been and would fight against the prince of Persia again. Then he said the prince of Greece would come. This is because in Daniel 2, Daniel had received understanding of the king's dream regarding the various kingdoms of government that would rise after Babylon. (Note: Persia today is Iran, and today the physical site of Babylon is Iraq.)

The Medes and Persians had taken over Babylon and were ruling. However, Greece would be the next ruling kingdom that would rise. The angel of the Lord knew that there would be a demonic spirit with that kingdom, which he called the prince of Greece. He then said that Michael, the Lord's prince (the strongest of all the angelic kingdom) would come to support him against these spirits when he left Daniel.

The prince of Persia and the prince of Greece were not earthly leaders. They were demonic spirits over that geographic land at the time. This scripture shows us that there have always been demonic spirits who seek to influence what governments do on earth. However, through prayer, speaking God's Word, worship, and obeying God's directions, God's people have been able to overcome these spirits time and time again as God sends His angelic help in difficult situations.

What we learn from this account of Daniel is not to fear, but to pray; to remain in faith and not quit praying. Our prayers and faith in God's Word assist God's angelic spirits to work in our behalf. Prayer is our communication line with God. It is like breathing. We have to keep breathing to live. Prayer should never be seen as just a quick fix or even as an obligation. It is our lifeline. Prayer is our place of power over the enemy.

Second Corinthians 10:4 says, "The weapons of our warfare are not carnal (of this natural realm), but mighty through God to the pulling down of strong holds."

The psalmist gave another weapon against the enemy, and that is our praise and worship to God.

Psalm 149:6–9 (NKJV) tells us that our praise to God binds the spirits of kings and nobles and brings judgment upon them. He wasn't talking about natural people. He was referring to spirit beings who manipulate people negatively.

In Matthew 21:16 Jesus quoted from Psalm 8:2, emphasizing that even out of the mouth of spiritual babes (newborn Christians), praise stills (has power over) the enemy and brings strength to God's people.

Second Chronicles, chapter 20, gives us a great example of this. When Jehoshaphat and the children of Israel were surrounded by enemies, they began to pray and then began to worship. It happened just as Scripture said. The enemies began to fight and destroy each other as Israel praised God. Operating in God's leading and His principles enables us to overcome no matter what we face here on earth.

As I mentioned in chapter three, in January 2008, my late husband and I were praying, and he told me, "I get in my spirit things are about to intensify." When he said this, I knew that sounded right, but I did not know that we would walk through a testing time fighting a spiritual battle against a sickness the following year and that my husband would be released to go home and be with the Lord. I became very aware during that time and afterward of the spiritual battle intensifying against believers around the world in many ways.

In those last few days of Billy Joe's life, as I shared earlier, he saw over into the spirit realm. On one occasion when I had stepped out of the room, he asked for one of our close friends to come near his bed and pray in tongues with strong prayer. He told him he saw fiery darts coming at him from every direction. Our friend began praying strong with Billy Joe, and then Billy Joe went back to sleep. After this, my husband became very aware of needing to communicate direction. Later, I wondered if he knew he could possibly be leaving us.

Before Billy Joe became hooked up to a lot of medical equipment where he couldn't communicate, he gave instructions on paper of his thoughts that I should step into the pulpit in his absence, and then he wrote that he realized the Board would need to approve this as well. I was not present when this happened. I was with him every day and night except a few times when I had to go to our home for a change of clothes or to prepare to speak.

He also called our Associate Pastor, as one of our ministry friends was listening, to tell him that he believed our son Paul was to be the future pastor, but was not yet ready at that time and he needed our Associate Pastor to be there to help with his transition when it would take place.

We had believed for Billy Joe's healing. Many were praying around the world at that point. When he passed away in that hospital room, I was determined to pray for his resurrection according to Hebrews 11:35 that by faith "women received their dead raised to life again...." I prayed for three hours and read scriptures on resurrection. I prayed in tongues and worshipped God.

As I began worshiping the Lord, I heard a choir of voices at a distance singing with me. I knew it was angels singing. Every time I breathed, they breathed. If I stopped, they stopped. I kept worshiping and listening to them singing with me.

I looked down at my husband's face, and he had a huge smile as he laid there with his eyes closed. Even his teeth were showing. I knew he was gone from his body and he was happy. He had entered into a rest from his labor on earth.

My husband worked hard while living on earth. I felt that he lived the life of two or three men in one body. He pushed himself because he had a sense of a mandate upon his life. While living on earth, he would sacrifice taking time for himself in order to benefit others, including our family. He always made time for the Lord and for God's Word. He just didn't do many other things for himself. I'm thankful for the years we had together here on earth. I learned spiritual principles from him that continue to help me in life.

> *Blessed are the dead which die in the Lord from henceforth…that they may rest from their labours; and their works do follow them.*
> —REVELATION 14:13

Looking back, I've thought about the last few years of his life. He was very focused on awakening people to be preparing for eternity. He had written articles about it called "Focused on Eternity," and had prepared a series about it.

When you become focused on eternity, it affects how you live your life here on earth. You know that one day you will stand before God and give an account of your life here on earth. You know that in that day you will get to see the fruit of your life as well here on earth.

Right before Billy Joe went into the hospital, he had just edited a transcript of a small book he felt people needed when a loved one dies. He had sent it back to our dear friend who assisted us with editing books. That transcript had been returned, and when we arrived at home after he had died, it was on our kitchen counter, ready to be published—"Victory Over Death." We had the book printed and gave out copies of it at his memorial service to the more than 10,000 people who attended. The printing company who printed it donated the cost of the books because of their love for my husband.

Billy Joe was led by the Lord to name the last building project that he was over, "Rising to a New Level," and as we were finishing it, he called the last phase, "Finishing Strong." We had always bought land and built debt-free through the years, releasing our faith for miracles, but that project was the biggest yet and God worked supernaturally, not just for the church, but for all who gave individually. It was quite a faith undertaking. Billy Joe prayed continually through that time—week to week as we believed for the finances to always pay our construction workers.

Throughout the years of our church and our personal lives, my husband and I saw the power of faith through agreement for everything God had called us to do. Billy Joe had kept his faith, and he had done what he was directed by God to do while here on earth.

In 2 Timothy 4:6–8 (NKJV), Paul the apostle came to a point where he sensed in his spirit:

> *The time of my departure is at hand. I have fought the good fight, I have finished the race, I have kept the faith. Finally, there is laid up for me the crown of righteousness, which the Lord the righteous Judge, will give me at that Day, and not to me only but also to all who have loved His appearing.*

As Billy Joe left his physical body to go to heaven (the third heaven), I believe he was drawn by the love of our Father to what Hebrews 11:16 (NKJV) says is a better country:

But now they desire a better, that is, a heavenly country.
Therefore God is not ashamed to be called their God, for He
has prepared a city for them.

Six weeks after Billy Joe died, I ministered with my brother at my
91-year-old father's memorial service. He had said he was ready to go.
Two years later, my little grandmother, who was over 102 years old,
passed away.

Before Grandmother passed, as I shared earlier, she had a dream
three times where she saw fiery missiles coming on earth from every
direction. The first time she had the dream, she thought that it was
an attack upon the U. S. However, the next two times she had the
dream she said she saw a map of countries of the world where the fiery
missiles were coming down upon them.

I told her that Billy Joe had had a similar dream before he passed
and that I believed she saw into the spirit realm too where the fiery
darts of the devil and his demons were coming at people on earth.

Ephesians 6:16 (NKJV) says, "Above all, taking the shield of faith
with which you will be able to quench all the fiery darts of the wicked
one." *The Amplified Bible* refers to the "fiery darts" as "flaming
missiles."

What are these flaming missiles? Everything that Satan can think
of to steal, kill, and destroy people—sickness and disease, depression,
mental illness, addictions to alcohol, drugs, pornography, and sexual
sin, such as fornication, homosexuality, and child abuse; anger that
abuses others, deception, fierce persecution against Christians, false
accusations, distractions toward other things so a person stops seeking
God; oftentimes, bitterness, murder, strife and division, an antichrist

spirit, and anti-Semitism; wars, natural disasters, such as storms and earthquakes, floods and famine, etc.

Revelation 12:12 says, "Woe to the inhabiters of the earth and of the sea! for the devil is come down unto you, having great wrath, because he knoweth he hath but a short time."

The devil knows that he and his demon spirits have an allotted time to be here on earth. We can see this in the Scripture of Matthew 8:28–29, which tells about two men possessed with devils who were exceedingly fierce. They came out of tombs and came at Jesus, crying, "What have we to do with You, Jesus, You Son of God? Have you come here to torment us *before the time*?" (v. 29, NKJV). These spirits knew who Jesus was. They feared Him, and they weren't sure if something had changed regarding their allotted time being able to move around on earth.

Revelation 20 tells the ultimate fate of the devil and his demons. When their time is up, they will be bound for a thousand years. Then the devil and his demons will be released at the end of the thousand years right before the great battle between Jesus Christ and His army and the army of Satan. Satan's army will be defeated, and they will be cast into the lake of fire and brimstone to be tormented day and night forever (Revelation 20:1–3, 7–10).

We've been given the shield of faith to stop the fiery missiles of the enemy. Faith is not just something we believe as a doctrine. Faith is an aggressive force that we've been given to use to overcome. We've been given the sword of the Spirit—our weapon against Satan—decreeing God's Word.

Faith in Jesus and in God's Word is our victory to overcome Satan and his fiery missiles. Jesus gave us victory over death, hell, and the grave (Revelation 1:18). When Jesus died and descended into the lower parts of the earth, He stripped Satan of his power (or authority) over mankind. He took the keys of hell and death from the devil, then rose victorious from the grave to ascend to the highest heaven (Ephesians 4:9–10; Colossians 2:15). He did not destroy the devil, but He took his authority from him.

Jesus gave us authority to use here on earth through His name, His blood, and His Word (Luke 10:19; Mark 13:33–37; 16:17–18; Matthew 28:18–20; Ephesians 1:16–23, 2:6).

Jesus rose victorious over Satan from the dead, and now sits at the right hand of God the Father where He prays for you and me (Ephesians 1:20; Hebrews 7:25). Jesus' victory over death and His resurrection empower us and deliver us from the fear of death.

We know that when we die, immediately we are transported to the highest heaven with Jesus and with others who have gone on before us. Rather than feeling defeat or loss when a Christian dies, we see victory in Jesus. Our faith helps us to live in victory, knowing none of Satan's devices can defeat us.

Those who pass into heaven immediately receive resurrected, immortal bodies, and they celebrate being in the presence of the Lord. They join in the cloud of witnesses who have gone on before us, and they are believing for us here on earth to finish our course with joy (Acts 20:24).

The world doesn't understand this sense of victory. They can't see beyond this life so they fall apart at the death of a loved one. They cling to this earthly life and fear what they don't know beyond the grave. God's Word and His Holy Spirit give us the assurance of our victory and eternity with Jesus.

> *"O Death, where is your sting? O Hades, where is your victory?" The sting of death is sin, and the strength of sin is the law. But thanks be to God who gives us the victory through our Lord Jesus Christ.*
> —1 CORINTHIANS 15:55–57 (NKJV)

Death has no sting, because we know where we are going when we leave our earthly body; and we are free from the effects of sin. The grave has no victory, because we have resurrection power living inside of us through Jesus Christ. We have victory through our Lord Jesus Christ.

Chapter 16

THE THIRD HEAVEN

The third and highest heaven is the heaven of heavens where God lives, where angels and the dead in Christ who have been redeemed from all nations are worshiping Him.

You're the one, God, you alone; you made the heavens, the heavens of heavens, and all angels; the earth and everything on it, the seas and everything in them; you keep them all alive; heaven's angels worship you! You're the one, God....
—Nehemiah 9:6–7 (msg)

What is heaven like? I have not been there personally, but I have read Scripture for over 44 years now, and Scripture gives us some insight about heaven. I have read stories of and spoken with those who have had experiences of going to heaven and returning to their bodies who have told about what they saw. One of these accounts was with Dr. Eben Alexander.

Testimony of Dr. Eben Alexander

On October 15, 2012, *Newsweek* magazine told of a true story of a neurosurgeon, Dr. Eben Alexander, who experienced life after death and returned to tell what happened.

Dr. Alexander had taught at Harvard Medical School and other medical universities, and at the time he was a neurosurgeon at Lynchburg General Hospital.

Dr. Alexander considered himself a Christian in name more than actual belief. He had believed that Jesus was a good man who suffered at the hands of wicked people. However, he said that he struggled with believing anything beyond that. He had heard some people tell stories of near-death experiences where they had actually left their bodies, went to heaven, and returned back into their bodies. He dismissed these stories as unreal and only hallucinations.

However, in the fall of 2008, something happened to him that changed his perspective. He awakened one morning with an extreme headache, and within hours he was in the hospital where he worked, diagnosed with a very rare bacterial meningitis that normally only had attacked some newborn babies. E-coli bacteria had penetrated his cerebrospinal fluid and was eating his brain. Doctors recorded that his first chance of survival was possibly a vegetative state, but later said it was worse because he appeared to show no hope at all for survival.

For seven days he lay in a deep coma. His body was not responsive, and his higher order brain functions were totally offline.

Dr. Alexander said that during this time, his conscious and inner self were alive and well. With his brain cortex completely shut down and his body under medical observation, he said that he left his body and began to journey upward first, seeing puffy pink-white clouds. He then continued to journey higher where he saw shimmering winged beings shooting across the sky, leaving streaming lines behind them.

Later, as he recalled this event, he thought it might have been birds or angels, but he said whatever they were, they seemed to be an advanced higher form of life. They had such a joy, they could not contain it.

Then he heard a huge booming sound of a glorious chant, and he wondered if the sound was coming from these beings because of their joy. The sound was like rain that he could feel, but he wasn't getting wet.

As he journeyed, he could see and hear the beings singing and making music with perfection. All of it made him want to join in singing with them. In fact, he said it seemed that he could not look at or listen to anything in this place without wanting to become a part of it.

Dr. Alexander shared how everything was connected or interwoven together. Nothing was separate. Throughout the journey, one of the beings was with him as they rode on something that appeared to be like a butterfly wing. As they went, millions of butterflies flew all around them like a river of life and color moving through the air.

Throughout his journey, he was accompanied by a young woman who was dressed very simple, but everything about her was so alive and colorful. She looked at him, not in a romantic way or just a friendship, but a higher form of love that was pure and holy. Without saying any words, she spoke to him and as the message went through him like a wind, he understood her. The message was, "You are loved and cherished dearly forever. You have nothing to fear. In this place, there is nothing you can do wrong."

Hearing this caused a sensation of relief. He said he felt as if he had been given the rules of life where as before he couldn't understand it. The being said, "We will show you many things here, but eventually you will go back."

He thought, "Back where?" Then a soft, warm wind blew through and each question he thought in his mind was answered by thoughts that were sent to him. There were concepts that he said would take him years to fully grasp in his earthly life that he understood effortlessly. As he continued to move forward, he came into an area that was completely dark, and a light came to guide him.

On the seventh day of his coma, doctors were about to decide to discontinue treatment when his eyes popped open.

As a medical scientist, Dr. Alexander knew that some suggest that these experiences are the result of minimal, transient, or partial malfunctioning of the cortex. However, he shared that his cortex was not malfunctioning but was totally off. This was evident from the severity of the meningitis and the documented neurological examinations. Medically speaking, it was impossible for him to have experienced even limited consciousness during his coma.

Dr. Alexander shared how his life has been forever changed. Before he thought that science was the way to truth, but now he knows that faith in God is. He shared, "I'm still a doctor and still a man of science every bit as much as I was before, but now I live with a deeper understanding of reality." (Dr. Alexander wrote his story in more detail in a book called, *Proof of Heaven*.)

* * *

The secular media has been intrigued by the accounts shared and has interviewed some of the people. However, they have also criticized them and even had psychologists on their programs to state their opinions, trying to discount the experiences as hallucinations of the mind. If these media people and psychologists lived in the days of Isaiah, Ezekiel, and the Apostle Paul or the Apostle John, they would discount those men and their experiences as well.

The accounts in the Bible are real, even though they are very unusual and beyond what mankind has seen with the natural eyes. God is beyond man's finite mind. He is infinite.

There are several accounts in the Bible where men saw into the highest heaven. Although I have previously referred to both Isaiah and Paul's experiences, I want to revisit these as well as the accounts of Ezekiel and the Apostle John: While one could not speak of the glory that he saw, three of these men described their experience.

Paul

> It is doubtless not profitable for me to boast. I will come to visions and revelations of the Lord: I know a man in Christ who fourteen years ago—whether in the body I do not know, or whether out of the body I do not know, God knows—such a one was caught up to the third heaven. And I know such a man—whether in the body or out of the body I do not know, God knows—how he was caught up into Paradise and heard inexpressible words, which it is not lawful for a man to utter.
>
> —2 CORINTHIANS 12:1–4 (NKJV)

Paul did not give the details of what he saw, but in the midst of the trials and the persecution he had experienced, as he sought the Lord he had a vision of the third heaven. It was so glorious that he wrote that he couldn't speak of all that he saw. Through Paul, we have the discovery and solid truth that there are three heavens.

Isaiah

> In the year that King Uzziah died, I saw the Lord sitting on a throne, high and lifted up, and the train of His robe filled the temple.
>
> Above it stood seraphim; each one had six wings: with two he covered his face, with two he covered his feet, and with two he flew.
>
> And one cried to another and said:
>
> "Holy, holy, holy is the LORD of hosts; the whole earth is full of His glory!"
>
> And the posts of the door were shaken by the voice of him who cried out, and the house was filled with smoke.
>
> So I said:
>
> "Woe is me, for I am undone! Because I am a man of unclean lips, and I dwell in the midst of a people of unclean lips; for my eyes have seen the King, the Lord of hosts."
>
> Then one of the seraphim flew to me, having in his hand a live coal which he had taken with the tongs from the altar.
>
> And he touched my mouth with it, and said: "Behold, this has touched your lips; your iniquity is taken away, and your sin purged."
>
> Also I heard the voice of the LORD, saying: "Whom shall I send, and who will go for Us?" Then I said, "Here am I! Send me."
>
> —ISAIAH 6:1–8 (NKJV)

As I mentioned in chapter 13, Isaiah was a young prophet at the time of this experience. He had served on the court of his cousin, King Uzziah. He starts this scripture by saying, "In the year that King Uzziah died." King Uzziah had been a great leader. He had restored the nation of Judah to greatness. He had built cities, water towers, and increased the agriculture of the land. He had dug wells. The country had become prosperous under his leadership because he had sought the Lord. He built a strong military, inventing engines for defense. Other nations recognized him as a strong leader. However, he became proud and disobeyed God's will. He would not repent. He was struck with leprosy and died.

Like many others, Isaiah grieved over Uzziah's death. Isaiah probably felt some insecurity about his role and about the future of the nation. He knew that countries bordering their land might attempt to attack when they heard that the king had died. In times past, they'd had confidence in King Uzziah's leadership, knowing he would lead them in victory. Now that he had died, there were possible questions about his 25-year-old son being able to rise and lead the nation in his place.

At this point, Isaiah sought the Lord, and as he did, he had a vision of heaven. He saw God on the throne, high and lifted up. (Note: Whenever someone dies whom people have depended on, God is still on His throne and still has a plan to take people forward.)

Around the throne of God were angels and spirit beings (seraphim) crying out, "Holy, holy, holy is the Lord of hosts..." (v. 3).

Isaiah felt humbled and convicted for his human sin nature. An angel took a hot coal and touched Isaiah's mouth, saying that his iniquity was cleansed. Then he heard the voice of the Lord say, "Who will go for us to the people and speak My words?" Isaiah replied, "Here am I! Send me" (v. 8).

Glimpses of God's Future Plan of Restoration

Isaiah later wrote that one day when the earth and heavens are restored to God's original plan, the wolf will dwell with the lamb; the leopard, the lion, and the bear will dwell with the cow and their young, and they will not devour them. Children will live around various animals, reptiles, insects, birds, and fish and not be harmed by them. None shall hurt or destroy others in heaven. This lets us see that heaven has animals and other living creatures that we have here on earth, but none of them harm one another (Isaiah 11:6–9).

Ezekiel

Ezekiel was another prophet of the Old Testament. He lived at the same time as Daniel, Shadrach, Meshach, and Abednego.

> *Now it came to pass in the thirtieth year, in the fourth month, on the fifth day of the month, as I was among the captives by the River Chebar, that the heavens were opened and I saw visions of God.*
> —Ezekiel 1:1 (NKJV)

Babylon ruled the earth and invaded Judah, destroying the temple of God. They burned down the walls surrounding Jerusalem and took King Jehoichin and many strong and educated young men captive, such as Ezekiel, moving them to Babylon.

In this time of great upheaval, Ezekiel prayed daily. He knew the prophecy that Jeremiah had spoken that there would be 70 years that the people of God would be in Babylon, but would one day return.

One day as Ezekiel was praying, suddenly he had a vision and saw into heaven. First, he saw a great storm from the north driving a huge cloud with fire inside of it, flashes of lightning around it, and a bright light. He saw four unusual celestial beings. They moved as quick as lightning. He saw a large wheel and a wheel inside of it as it moved quickly with the celestial beings. Then he saw the Lord sitting upon His throne of heavenly blue surrounded with bright light that had the appearance of fire and a rainbow. After seeing this, he heard the voice of God speaking to him. The Lord gave him understanding of the future and what he was to speak to God's people.

Today psychologists would probably consider Ezekiel's vision a hallucination. However, when you read the vision that the apostle John received on the Isle of Patmos, you see some similarities. God gave Ezekiel and John visions of heaven because He wanted His people to know that heaven is real, that there is a spiritual battle going on, that there are future events that will happen to fulfill prophecy, and that one day there will be a new heaven and a new earth.

In both Isaiah and Ezekiel's accounts, the Lord asked them to be the messenger to speak His word to the people.

John

> I was in the Spirit on the Lord's Day, and I heard behind me a loud voice, as of a trumpet."
>
> —REVELATION 1:10 (NKJV)

Then as I looked, I saw a door standing open in heaven, and
the same voice I had heard before spoke to me like a trumpet
blast. The voice said, "Come up here, and I will show you what
must happen after this." And instantly I was in the Spirit,
and I saw a throne in heaven and someone sitting on it. The
one sitting on the throne was as brilliant as gemstones—like
jasper and carnelian. And the glow of an emerald circled his
throne like a rainbow. Twenty-four thrones surrounded him,
and twenty-four elders sat on them. They were all clothed in
white and had gold crowns on their heads. From the throne
came flashes of lightning and the rumble of thunder. And in
front of the throne were seven torches with burning flames.
This is the sevenfold Spirit of God. In front of the throne was
a shiny sea of glass, sparkling like crystal.
—REVELATION 4:1–6 (NLT)

In Revelation 21, John describes the holy city of heaven—Jerusalem. There is a great wall that surrounds it, and it has twelve foundations with precious gems embedded in each foundation. There were twelve gates made of pearl as entrances into the city. These gates are never shut.

The city is a series of mountains, starting with low foothills just inside the walls. For 1,500 miles the city ascends to the highest mountain where the heavenly dwelling place of God is, and worship surrounds the throne as Revelation, chapters 4 and 5, describe.

There is a pure river of water of life, clear as crystal that comes out of the throne of God. On both sides of the river there is the tree of life with leaves and fruit that have healing power in them.

There was no more curse as there had been on earth, no sickness, no pain, no abuse, no sin, no suffering, no evil of any kind. There were living fountains of water throughout the city.¹⁷ John saw the streets made of gold.

God and His throne are in the highest heaven!

> *For He looked down from the height of His sanctuary; from heaven the Lord viewed the earth.*
>
> —Psalm 102:19 (NKJV)

> *He will hear him from his holy heaven with the saving strength of his right hand.*
>
> —Psalm 20:6

> *The Lord's throne is in heaven....*
>
> —Psalm 11:4

> *God reigns over the nations; God sits upon His holy throne.*
>
> —Psalm 47:8 (AMP)

God never gets off of His throne. He is there to reign. That lets us know that nothing that happens on earth removes Him from His reigning position. He reigns forever over every situation.

> *I looked, and behold, a great multitude which no one could number, of all nations, tribes, peoples, and tongues, standing before the throne and before the Lamb, clothed with white robes, with palm branches in their hands.*
>
> —Revelation 7:9 (NKJV)

This is just one scene of the activity that goes on in heaven. There is more going on.

---

17 Ibid., 303–304.

An Account of Today

I remember visiting with a couple in our church whose brother had just passed away. They had prayed and believed for his healing. He was married and had a teenage daughter who had recently graduated from school. They had been very close as a family. The wife and daughter had believed for him to live and remain on earth.

In the hospital, at one point he flatlined and left his physical body. He went to heaven but returned back into his body. Suddenly he sat up in his bed and told his wife and daughter, "Hey, Honey and Chelsey, it's not like you think. It's wonderful! I was so happy. They were just discussing my assignment."

Then he boldly prayed, "Lord Jesus, thank You for this glorious day. Thank You for what You have for me today and for tomorrow, and I thank You for these two beautiful women You have in my life. Amen!"

Then he asked, "Where is my Bible?" His wife asked him, "Did you see Jesus?" He replied, "Yes, and everything else."

He died not long after this. Of course, his wife and daughter wanted him to remain here on earth, but he saw over to the other side and was drawn there.

> *The First Man was made out of earth, and people since then are earthy; the Second Man was made out of heaven, and people now can be heavenly. In the same way that we've worked from our earthy origins, let's embrace our heavenly ends.*
>
> —1 CORINTHIANS 15:47–49 (MSG)

Bruce got a glimpse of eternity in heaven and embraced his heavenly end. I am convinced from the stories I have heard regarding life after death experiences that people feel so wonderful they do not want to return to their earthly physical condition, even though they love their family members very much.

Qualities of the Third Heaven

Joy

There are many qualities or aspects of heaven. One is joy. There is fullness of joy in heaven. Those who have gone to heaven and returned to their physical bodies say that they felt a joy that is beyond description. Psalm 16:11 (NKJV) says, "In Your presence is fullness of joy...."

While people may grieve at the passing of a loved one, that loved one is not grieving. Instead, he or she is happy and celebrating being in the presence of God, knowing that they made it to their eternal home. I would imagine there is praise and gratitude upon arriving there.

Jude 24 (CEV) says, "Offer praise to God our Savior because of our Lord Jesus Christ! Only God can keep you from falling and make you pure and joyful in his glorious presence."

The greatest joy will be in seeing Jesus, our Savior, who gave His sinless life on the cross and paid the price for us to be delivered from Satan and the power of sin. Jesus' resurrection enables us to be raised from death to life while living on earth, giving us a newness of life. But even greater than this is that we are resurrected from death to life when we die. Praise God! All of this is because of His love, His forgiveness, His mercy and grace, because we could never earn it ourselves by trying to be good on our own.

There is joy in having a new resurrected body. There is no sickness, no weakness, nothing lacking of body parts, no aging, no mental illness, no suffering or pain, no addictions, no brokenness. Instead, there is complete soundness, wholeness, peace, and freedom.

First Corinthians 15:51 says, "We shall all be changed." Verses 43–44 in the *New Living Translation* say, "Our bodies are buried in brokenness, but they will be raised in glory. They are buried in weakness, but they will be raised in strength. They are buried as natural human bodies, but they will be raised as spiritual bodies. For just as there are natural bodies, there are also spiritual bodies."

Another joy will be seeing loved ones from the past who have gone on to their heavenly home before us. We will see people that we knew and people that we didn't know on earth whose lives were changed through our life touching them in some way in giving, praying, or through our witnessing to them in brief moments on earth. We will hear their stories and rejoice at how God divinely connected our lives on earth, enabling them to hear the gospel message and be saved.

There will be joy as we enter into God's rewards for any labor that we did or any prayers that we prayed on earth that resulted in people being saved, rescued, discipled, healed, or delivered from the enemy.

Bright Light

Another aspect or quality of heaven is light. Heaven is filled with light that comes from God Himself.

There is no darkness in the third heaven. Revelation 22:5 (NKJV) says, "There shall be no night there: They need no lamp nor light of the sun, for the Lord God gives them light...." Revelation 21:23 describes heaven in the same way: "The city had no need of the sun or of the moon to shine in it, for the glory of God illuminated it. The Lamb is its light."

Love

God's presence is love! Therefore, love fills heaven.

> *God is love... and he that dwelleth in love dwelleth in God, and God in him.*
>
> —1 JOHN 4:8, 16

Love that goes beyond human understanding is in heaven. It is holy and pure, cleansing, liberating, healing, forgiving, affirming, merciful, compassionate, caring, safe, secure, and abundant to all who go to heaven. We will be so grateful for God's love and humbled by the love that God has for us when we arrive in heaven.

> *But God demonstrates his own love for us in this: While we were still sinners, Christ died for us.*
> *Since we have now been justified by his blood, how much more shall we be saved from God's wrath through him!*
>
> —ROMANS 5:8–9 (NIV)

Jesus Is in Heaven!

Jesus is the main focus in heaven. He is the Lamb who is able to open the Book of Life that has been sealed.

Jesus, our Savior, God's only Son, the Lamb who was slain to bear the sins of the world on the cross, took the keys of hell and of death and rose victorious from the dead.

> *It is Christ who died, and furthermore is also risen, who is even at the right hand of God, who also makes intercession for us.*
>
> —ROMANS 8:34 (NKJV)

> *He is able, once and forever, to save those who come to God through him. He lives forever to intercede with God on their behalf.*
>
> —HEBREWS 7:25 (NLT)

Jesus intercedes (prays for you and me) while we are here on earth. I am grateful for His prayers!

Jesus is also our Advocate. "And if anyone sins, we have an Advocate with the Father, Jesus Christ the righteous" (1 John 2:1, NKJV). Our Advocate is a lawyer of defense when Satan, the opposing lawyer, comes with accusations against us in heaven's court. Jesus is our Advocate when we have kept ourselves submitted to Jesus' authority (James 4:7), and when we are quick to confess to Him when we know we have done wrong (1 John 1:9). Jesus reminds the devil of His blood in and around our lives. He is standing in the gap for us, defending us.

All of the redeemed will be in heaven. That is, all who have believed in and received Jesus as Lord and Savior on earth. "For thou [Jesus] wast slain, and hast redeemed us to God by thy blood out of every kindred, and tongue, and people, and nation" (Revelation 5:9). When we arrive in heaven, we will understand fully how that in Jesus Christ we are all one blood, not various people groups. (See Acts 17:26.)

There won't be separated groups of people in heaven, no racial grouping, no denominational grouping; no youth hanging out in one area and adults hanging out in another area; no age group separation; no different language groups. Remember, originally people spoke the same language on earth. It wasn't until the Tower of Babel that languages separated people.

In heaven we will all speak the same language. I'm not sure what that language will be, but we will understand each other.

I find it interesting that many of the testimonies I have heard of people dying, going to heaven, and then returning to their bodies, say that they didn't even speak most of the time when they were in that heavenly realm. Instead, they communicated by thoughts. They would think a thought and the Spirit being with them would answer their thought with a thought. Whatever form of communication there is in heaven, it will be accepted by everyone. There are no independent attitudes, resistance, or rebellion in heaven. Everyone submits to God's authority so there is perfect unity in heaven.

Heaven Is Holy

Heaven has an atmosphere that is holy because God is holy! "The Lord is in his holy temple; the Lord sits on his throne in heaven. He sees what people do; he keeps his eye on them" (Psalm 11:4, NCV).

"Exalt ye the Lord our God, and worship at his footstool; for he is holy" (Psalm 99:5).

Some people have difficulty with the word *holy*, because religion has made it a legalistic form rather than a yieldedness of the heart where God is given freedom and power to rule over your thoughts, words, attitudes, and actions.

In the Hebrew language "holy" is *qadosh,* which is something dedicated to God, morally clean and consecrated to Him. In the Greek, it is *hagios,* which means set apart for sacred use; free from sin; pure, consecrated to God, something hallowed as very precious.

God is holy. He has no sin. He desires us to be like Him. On earth we have been given freedom of choice. When we choose Jesus to be our Lord and Savior, "Lord" means ruler. He doesn't force us to do anything, but He knows that if we are planning to go to heaven, we learn to live under His authority while we are on earth. In heaven, there is no sin, no evil, nothing unholy. Sometimes we think that because sin is all around us on earth that God is okay with sin. God was never okay with sin. It's why He sent His Son to earth to die and pay the price for our sin to be remitted and for us to allow Him to rule over our lives. When we go to heaven, there will be nothing unholy.

Chapter 17

GREAT EXPECTATION FOR WHAT IS AHEAD

Your faith and love continue because you know what is waiting for you in heaven—the hope you have had since you first heard the true message, the Good News that was told you....

—Colossians 1:5–6 (ERV)

It is by his great mercy that we have been born again, because God raised Jesus Christ from the dead. Now we live with great expectation, and we have a priceless inheritance—an inheritance that is kept in heaven for you....

—1 Peter 1:3–4 (NLT)

WHEN PETER WROTE THAT we live with great expectation, he didn't have any doubt about "heaven being for real"! He accepted the words of the prophets and the words of Jesus. He had friends who had had experiences of seeing heaven and talking about it—friends like Paul (2 Corinthians 12:1–4) and John (who wrote the book of Revelation). He and the other disciples had seen and spoken with Jesus after He had been raised from the dead, ascended to heaven, and had returned in a glorified body.

Peter knew what Stephen had spoken of his vision when he was dying and had seen the heavens open and Jesus standing on the right hand of God (Acts 7:56). This is why Peter wrote that we can live with great expectation for what is ahead of us. He knew heaven is the destiny of everyone who believes and surrenders his or her life to Jesus Christ.

A word for "anticipate"—as to anticipate your real home in heaven—is to expect. To expect means you can believe what you have been told. Because of Jesus making the way for us through giving His life on the cross and being raised from the dead, He has promised if we will believe in Him and accept His lordship in our lives, we will be saved from hell and thus go to heaven when we die.

This means we can anticipate a hope and a future beyond death because of Jesus—heaven. That's why we know "our best days are ahead of us." Heaven is what we have a great expectation of when the time comes for us to leave this earthly body and go into eternity.

Peter says we have a priceless inheritance ahead. Our inheritance is first of all Jesus Himself. We will be overwhelmed with His love when we arrive in heaven. We will inherit everything that Jesus provided through the cross and His resurrection—fullness of life, no sin, no temptation, no struggles or trials, no evil, no fear, no suffering, no sickness, nothing missing, nothing broken, wholeness, no tears, no pain, no torment or depression, and no lack of anything.

There will be fullness of joy, peace, love, rest, freedom, abundance of everything you could ever imagine and the most beautiful landscape surrounding you. You will have all the time you need (all eternity) to visit with people who have touched your life and people you have never touched as well. You will get to be with family members and friends you have known through the years. It will be a family reunion.

There will be rewards for those who have obeyed the Lord while on earth, being willing to take what they were given and multiply God's Kingdom here on earth.

The Root of All Fear

Years ago, I remember listening to a friend of ours, Pastor Tommy Barnett of Phoenix, Arizona, as he shared an incident that happened when he pastored in Davenport, Iowa.

Several pornography businesses opened up around his city. Realizing the devastating effects it would have on many who could become taken by the porn industry, he led a campaign of ministers and congregations to stand against it, pushing to have those businesses removed from the city. He began exposing certain people who were financing it.

During this time he and his family had their lives threatened. He was put on a hit list. On one occasion his wife was followed in her car by some men who were planning to harm her, but she escaped through an angelic intervention.

A television network interviewed Pastor Tommy one day and asked him, "Aren't you afraid of being killed?" He looked right into the camera and smiled, saying, "You can't scare a Christian with heaven."

Wow! That kind of response doesn't just come without spending time in prayer and meditating God's Word, allowing God's presence to fill your mind with His promises.

When a Christian has taken the time to search their soul and then release their faith in God's Word, the spirit of fear cannot paralyze them. Pastor Barnett had come to a place of realization that he did not have to live in fear of man and that his life was in God's hands, not man's hands.

The greatest fear a person has is the fear of death. Hebrews 2:14–15 tells us that through Jesus' death on the cross and His resurrection from the grave, He destroyed (abolished, rendered inactive) the power that the devil had held over God's people through fear. Jesus took our sin and through His redeeming blood, He set us free and we have victory over sin and death as well. In Him we have resurrection life and eternal life.

Paul wrote in 1 Corinthians 15:54–57 (NLT):

> *Then, when our dying bodies have been transformed into bodies that will never die, this Scripture will be fulfilled: "Death is swallowed up in victory. O death, where is your victory? O death, where is your sting?" For sin is the sting that results in death . . . But thank God! He gives us victory over sin and death through our Lord Jesus Christ.*

We don't have to fear death when we know we are right with God through faith in the blood of Jesus Christ. We know where we are going when we leave this earth life.

Fear is a spirit. We are told in 2 Timothy 1:7 (NKJV), "God has not given us a spirit of fear, but of power (*dunamis*—mighty strength, ability, and miraculous power), and of love and of a sound (a disciplined and controlled) mind." He told us that He left us with His authority, while here on earth, over the enemy (Satan). We can take authority over the spirit of fear and command it to leave us in Jesus' name. Then speak the scriptures of faith and peace over our lives. Our words have an effect upon what happens in our lives.

> *You will have to live with the consequence of everything you say. What you say can preserve life or destroy it; so you must accept the consequences of your words.*
> —PROVERBS 18:20–21 (GNT)

We can change our lives by changing the words we speak. We can begin to speak according to what God's Word says instead of speaking fear, doubt, or every negative thought that comes our way. We can train our thoughts by training our words.

Sometimes people fear the unknown or what lies ahead. They wonder what happens to a person when he or she dies. When we read Scripture, we don't have to be afraid.

First, when a believer dies who has committed his or her life to Jesus Christ, they are immediately taken into the presence of the Lord at the moment of death.

"To be absent from the body [is] to be present with the Lord" (2 Corinthians 5:8, NKJV). That is the greatest place of refuge—comfort, wholeness, love, and peace.

Second, when someone dies, they don't cease to exist!

When a Christian dies, they don't cease to exist. They just move from one location to another—from earth to heaven.

Jesus said in John 11:25–26 (NKJV):

"I am the resurrection and the life. He who believes in Me, though he may die, he shall live. And whoever lives and believes in Me shall never die...."

Although our physical body ceases to exist, the real part of us continues to live. This is why it is important to realize we are spirit, soul, and body. First Thessalonians 5:23 (NKJV) says, "May your whole spirit, soul, and body be preserved blameless at the coming of our Lord Jesus Christ." Then, Hebrews 4:12 (NIV) says, "For the word of God is alive and active. Sharper than any double-edged sword, it penetrates even to dividing soul and spirit, joints and marrow; it judges the thoughts and attitudes of the heart."

These two scriptures show us the separation of soul and spirit.

When I was growing up, I always thought the soul and spirit were the same. I didn't read the Bible, so I heard people using these two words interchangeably. When I began to read and study God's Word, I remember when I discovered that these two parts of me were not the same.

I heard someone teach on the subject, and it answered questions I had had regarding why some people receive the Lord but go back into bondage to sin or sometimes they just give into the lies of the devil and accept what he says.

The spirit is the part of us that becomes born again when we pray and ask Jesus into our heart. The soul is our mind, thoughts, and reasoning, our emotions, and our will or the part of us that reasons and makes choices.

People sometimes wonder after they receive Jesus why they still struggle with their thought life. The answer is they still have an unrenewed mind. I need to say this. You are not whatever sin you have been in bondage to. When you receive Jesus, you receive a new identity. However, you must renew your mind to God's Word. You have to attack the bondage of sin with the sword of His Spirit. You have to read, study, meditate, memorize, and speak what God's Word says.

When we choose to make time to put God's Word in our hearts, our view of life changes. Our reasoning becomes better. Our emotions begin to be brought under control rather than being out of control. We begin to want God's will to be done in our lives instead of demanding our will to be done.

The SPIRIT is:

The inner man within us.

Ephesians 3:16 (NKJV)—

"That He would grant you, according to the riches of His glory, to be strengthened with might through His Spirit in the inner man."

The new man.

Colossians 3:10 (NKJV)—

And have put on the new man who is renewed in knowledge according to the image of Him who created him."

The hidden man of the heart.

First Peter 3:4 (NKJV)—

"Rather let it be the hidden person of the heart, with the incorruptible beauty of a gentle and quiet spirit, which is very precious in the sight of God."

The SOUL is:

The mind (your reasoning), the will (your ability to choose or reject), and the emotions.

Romans 12:2 (NKJV)—

"Be transformed by the renewing of your mind...."

Ephesians 4:23 (NKJV)—

"And be renewed in the spirit of your mind."

The BODY is:

The physical part of you that people see.

Romans 12:1 (ESV)—

"Present your bodies as a living sacrifice, holy and acceptable to God, which is your spiritual worship."

First Corinthians 6:19 (NKJV)—

"Your body is the temple of the Holy Spirit who is in you...."

Second Corinthians 4:16 (NKJV)—

"Even though our outward man is perishing, yet the inward man is being renewed day by day."

At death, the physical, outward part of a person turns to dust (Job 34:15), but the inner man (the spirit) and soul of the person continue to exist. People who have shared beyond death experiences say that they still can feel, see, and think. They still had emotions and reasoning. This goes along with Luke 16:19–31 where Jesus told the story of two men. This wasn't a parable; it was a true story. One man was rich; the other was a beggar.

The beggar went to Paradise while the rich man went to hell. The rich man could still feel, think, and talk. He asked if the beggar could come touch his tongue with water, because he was in extreme thirst and torment in the flames around him. He was told that Lazarus, the beggar, could not cross over the dividing gulf between them. So the rich man asked if Moses could be sent back to earth from the dead and warn his brothers so they wouldn't go to hell. He was told "no," because his brothers had not believed the living people around them; and they would choose not to believe even if Moses appeared to them.

Third, what about people who were not willing to accept Jesus Christ as Lord and Savior?

Those who choose not to receive Jesus as Lord and Savior on earth will also continue to exist, except the Scripture says they will be in hell.

Some have said that if we don't accept Jesus Christ as Lord and Savior here on earth that after we die we go to a place where we are given a second chance to accept Him. This doesn't agree with Scripture. Others who have embraced the Hindu faith believe that when a person dies they will come back to earth again in another form for another chance to live on earth. Again, this doesn't agree with Scripture.

Hebrews 9:27 (NKJV) says, "It is appointed for men to die once, but after this the judgment." Mark 16:16 says, "He that believeth and is baptized shall be saved; but he that believeth not shall be damned."

Some people think hell will be a big party for the wicked. In reality, Jesus and the prophets have told us that hell will be a place, first of all, where there is the absence of God's presence, which means the absence of all hope. It will be a place of:

- Pits of gloom and chains of darkness/utter darkness— 2 Peter 2:4; Jude 12–13.
- Flames of fire—Luke 16:24.
- A lake of fire that burns with sulfur or brimstone— Revelation 19:20, 20:10, 21:8.
- Eternal fire/fire that is never quenched/where the worm never dies—Matthew 25:41; Mark 9:43–48.
- Torment forever/torment day and night forever— Revelation 14:11, 20:10.
- Everlasting punishment—Matthew 25:46.
- Shame and everlasting contempt—Daniel 12:2.
- Eternal destruction and the absence of the presence of God—2 Thessalonians 1:5–9. You are captive forever. There is no escape.
- Wailing (screaming) and gnashing of teeth/a furnace of fire—Matthew 13:42. Among those who will be there: the fearful, unbelieving, abominable, murderers, whoremongers, sorcerers, idolaters, and liars—Revelation 21:8.

Jesus said in the account of Luke 16:19–31 that the rich man went to hell and could still see and communicate. Hell was not created for mankind, but for the devil and his angels (Matthew 25:41), the future prison of the devil and his angels.

However, God gave mankind a free will, the ability to choose God and His ways or to reject Him. Those who reject Him cannot go where He is—heaven. In this way, God would know that man chose to love Him and was not simply forced to love Him.

Once Jesus came to earth to die for our sins and be raised from the dead for us, our way to God became through Jesus. We choose heaven or hell by what we do with Jesus. If we reject Jesus, we reject heaven, because He said that He is the only way to the Father (John 14:6).

When Jesus told this story, He had not yet gone to the cross to die and be raised up from the dead. Those who had believed in God and put their trust in Him for salvation, went to a place called Abraham's bosom to wait for Jesus, the Messiah, to come and raise them up with Him to heaven.

Jesus related that Lazarus, the beggar, who had put his faith in God, went to Abraham's bosom, a place of comfort, and enjoyed the blessings of abundance that he didn't have on earth.

Fourth, heaven has houses for us to live in.

We won't be floating on clouds or homeless. Jesus said He has prepared a home for us. John 14:1–3 (NKJV) says:

> *"Let not your heart be troubled; you believe in God, believe also in Me. In My Father's house are many mansions;* (the Orthodox Jewish Bible says dwelling places, permanent residences, homes) *if it were not so, I would have told you. I go to prepare a place for you. And if I go and prepare a place*

for you, I will come again and receive you to Myself; that
where I am, there you may be also."

Fifth, Jesus said that He will receive us to Himself when we die (see John 14:3, NKJV).

Some well-meaning people who didn't stop to consider the misunderstanding they would create about God have said at times, "God took your loved one" (a mother, father, wife, or child, etc.). People who have heard this who don't know the Lord have oftentimes resented God and blamed Him for taking their loved one from them. Some have said that they never wanted to step into a church again after their loved one died.

I believe it's important to see in the Scripture that Jesus said that He would "receive" a person in heaven, not "take them." Jesus said He came to give life, not take it, while the devil comes to steal, kill, and destroy (John 10:10).

Sometimes people die at a younger age, and people have mistakenly said statements like, "God needed another angel in heaven or another flower in His garden." Those statements are wrong. We don't become angels when we die, and we don't become flowers when we die. We are still people, and at death we receive glorified bodies.

God is not an unpredictable Father. Some say, "Well, God is omnipotent, and He chooses to do as He thinks best." They say everything that happens is God's will. However, Scripture tells us we are in a battle against an enemy who tries to rob the will and purpose of God in people's lives while they are on earth. We must never forget God's character, that He is a loving Father. He is not our problem. He is our help and our refuge.

In this spiritual battle, scripture tells us we can overcome the demonic spirits who seek to stop us from fulfilling God's plans and purposes, with the power of God. We can take authority over them in Jesus' name. We need to know that God is on our side. When the time comes for us to pass from this life to heaven, Jesus is there to receive us and embrace us with His love and affirmation.

Sixth, we will see and know our loved ones, friends, and other people when we get to heaven.

"I shall know, even as I also am known" (1 Corinthians 13:12, MEV). Some people wonder if we will know loved ones who died years ago. We will immediately know people around us and they will know us, whether they were children or adults when they died.

Seventh, what will we look like in heaven?

We will have resurrected, immortal bodies. (See 2 Corinthians 5:1–5 (MSG) and 1 Corinthians 15:48–54.) Jesus had a resurrected, glorified body when He came back to earth to visit the disciples, and He even ate a meal with them. (See Luke 24:42–43.) The disciples recognized Jesus. We will be recognizable as well.

The psalmist wrote that the Lord will renew our youth as the eagle's (Psalm 103:5). Those lacking parts of the body will be made whole (Psalm 139:16). There is a book of all your body parts for you to be made whole. Our bodies will have supernatural ability that we don't have in earthly bodies. We also will be able to walk through doors as if they weren't there. (In John 20:19, 26 Jesus came through doors that were shut.)

Eighth, we cannot escape eternity in heaven or hell.

Heaven is a literal country (a literal place), and hell is a literal place. We live in a time where there are deceivers who say heaven and hell are not real places, but that these words are figures of speech. They say heaven is what is experienced on earth, and hell is what is experienced on earth. For example, when people have a good life, they say it's "heaven on earth." Then, when people have a difficult life, they say they have "hell on earth."

Several years ago I happened to see a television talk show where the host of the program announced she was starting a new religion. I teach a course in Victory Bible College on "Avoiding Deception," so I wanted to hear what she was about to say.

Her guest that day was a "guru" on this new religion. At one point, she asked him if he thought about the afterlife, and he responded, "I don't give it much thought." He went on to say that he believed heaven and hell are not real places, but instead were what people experienced while living here on earth. He believed that there was no afterlife and that when a person dies, that's it, that there is nothing beyond the grave. What this belief promotes is that you can live your life on earth however you want with no concern about life after death.

Another deception of this belief that there is no afterlife is that it gives a person who may be in great pain or struggle the thought that they can end the pain and struggle by taking their life and that there will be no consequences after death.

Don't mistakenly fall for that deception, that when you die you cease to exist. You will continue to be very much alive, except you will have changed locations. Those who accept this lie are in danger of an afterlife that is not in heaven.

Proverbs 15:11 (NKJV) says, "Hell and destruction are before the Lord; so how much more the hearts of the sons of men." Matthew 10:28 (NKJV) says, "Do not fear those who kill the body but cannot kill the soul. But rather fear Him who is able to destroy both soul and body in hell."

We must realize there are those who seek to deceive others. There is only one way to avoid these deceptions and that is to stay committed to studying the Scriptures.

Second Timothy 3:13–16 (AMP) says:

> But wicked men and imposters will go from bad to worse, deceiving and leading astray others and being deceived and led astray themselves.
>
> But as for you, continue to hold to the things that you have learned and of which you are convinced, knowing from whom you learned [them].
>
> And how from your childhood you have had a knowledge of and been acquainted with the sacred Writings, which are able to instruct you and give you the understanding for salvation which comes through faith in Christ Jesus [through the leaning of the entire human personality on God in Christ Jesus in absolute trust and confidence in His power, wisdom, and goodness].
>
> Every Scripture is God-breathed (given by His inspiration) and profitable for instruction, for reproof and conviction of sin, for correction of error and discipline in obedience, [and] for training in righteousness (in holy living, in conformity to God's will in thought, purpose, and action).

Another Country

Hebrews 11:13–16 (GW) says:

> *All these people died having faith. They didn't receive the things that God had promised them, but they saw these things coming in the distant future and rejoiced. They acknowledged that they were living as strangers with no permanent home on earth.*
>
> *Those who say such things make it clear that they are looking for their own country.*
>
> *If they had been thinking about the country that they had left, they could have found a way to go back.*
>
> *Instead, these men were longing for a better country—a heavenly country. That is why God is not ashamed to be called their God. He has prepared a city for them.*

There is a heavenly country that is better than the country we have been living in here on earth, and there is a city there that we are all headed toward.

Hebrews 13:14 (NLT) says, "For this world is not our permanent home; we are looking forward to a home yet to come."

Philippians 3:20 (NKJV) says, "For our citizenship is in heaven, from which we also eagerly wait for the Savior, the Lord Jesus Christ."

These scriptures clearly indicate that we as Christians are from another country called heaven and that we are headed toward that heavenly country. You came from heaven to earth by birth through your mother's womb. In fact, Jeremiah 1:5 (NLT) says, "I (God) knew you before I formed you in your mother's womb...."

Every child born into this world came from God in heaven. When we come into this world, Ecclesiastes 3:11 (AMP) tells us that God has "planted eternity in men's hearts and minds [a divinely implanted sense of a purpose working through the ages which nothing under the sun but God alone can satisfy]...."

This awareness is to cause people to seek God to know Him. The enemy, Satan, attempts to distract and deceive people from seeking the one true God who created them. Without God directing their lives, people wander while they live on earth. It is why philosophers have asked the question through the centuries, "Why am I here? What is my purpose?"

First, when you don't know your Creator personally and you haven't allowed His Son, Jesus, to come into your heart, you will never answer those two questions in your own mind. Secondly, God reveals His will, His thoughts and ways to us in His Word—the Bible. Thirdly, the Holy Spirit who comes into a person when they are born again is in you to reveal answers to your questions and to guide you into knowing Truth.

Realizing that people need to know Him, we as Christians are called to tell others God's message of salvation and life.

God has us here as ambassadors representing His Kingdom and country as we live here on earth (2 Corinthians 5:19–20). An ambassador is someone on temporary assignment living in and representing another government of the country they are in, and they are there as reconcilers. An ambassador is taken care of by his or her country while they are living in a foreign land.

Jesus also told a parable in Luke 19:13 about a nobleman who took a journey and left money with those working for him, telling them to "occupy till I come." When a military occupies a place, they are there to bring authority, order, and stability. They are to keep an enemy from trying to come back in to oppress people. We are here as Christians to occupy where we are.

God wants us to use our authority to bring His order and stability in the places we live, to deliver people from the oppression of the devil, and to reach more people to go to heaven while we are here. We are here on temporary duty assignment. Second Timothy 1:9 tells us we have been saved and called "with an holy calling, not according to our works, but according to his own purpose and grace...." He has us on earth to live out His purpose, and He gives us the grace (divine empowerment) to do whatever He assigns us to do.

When God brings people into this world, He also gives each person the freedom of choice. If we choose to seek God and receive Jesus as Lord and Savior, when we die we return to the country we came from—heaven.

Those who don't receive Jesus as Lord and Savior are destined to eternal death (eternal separation from God) and damnation. "He that believeth and is baptized shall be saved; but he that believeth not shall be damned" (Mark 16:16).

I know that it is a hard statement, but God doesn't want people in heaven who do not want to be with Him. Hebrews 10:39 MEV says, "But we are not of those who draw back to destruction, but of those who have faith to the saving of the soul."

Proverbs 15:24 (GNT) says, "Wise people walk the road that leads upward to life, not the road that leads downward to death."

The enemy seeks to deceive people. He creates diversions to get people to take the wrong path. He brings distractions to stop us along the way. If we choose to take time with the Lord in His Word, prayer, and worship, seeking to know Him, He gives us His wisdom and helps us make right choices so we end up where we need to be—heaven!

Chapter 18

THE DRAW
OF HEAVEN

URING THE FIRST WEEK following my husband's passing, God spoke the word *trust* to me. I knew to trust in God with what I did not have full understanding of at that moment. I knew over time I would be able to see things more clearly.

That brings me to the purpose of this book. I believe when a Christian gets close to death, there is a draw of heaven upon his or her life that many times draws them over into eternity. Heaven is so far beyond what we experience here on earth. We tend to hang on to life here on earth, because it is what we are familiar with.

As I have read the accounts of people who have died, gone to heaven, and come back into their bodies, each of them has described heaven as so amazing that they didn't want to return, but were told they had to come back. Once they returned, they had a sense of urgency to tell people about heaven and to give their lives to Jesus.

Scripture encourages us not to seek to die. In fact, the psalmist makes a strong statement of faith in Psalm 118:17 (NKJV): "I shall not die, but live, and declare the works of the Lord."

David had enemies that wanted to kill him. He knew, of course, that one day he would die physically, but he also had an awareness of fulfilling God's purpose while living on earth and he knew that purpose had not yet been complete.

Acts 13:36 (NET) says, "For David, after he had served God's purpose in his own generation, died, was buried with his ancestors...."

I believe it is possible to know when you have fulfilled God's purpose here on earth. Paul wrote in Philippians 1:22 that he felt pulled between going to heaven to be with Christ and staying on earth with the people he had reached and was teaching at the time.

Later, he wrote in a letter to Timothy that he felt he had finished his course, had kept the faith, and was ready whenever his time would be to go to heaven.

> *For I am already being poured out as a drink offering, and the time of my departure is at hand.*
>
> *I have fought the good fight, I have finished the race, I have kept the faith.*
>
> *Finally, there is laid up for me the crown of righteousness, which the Lord, the righteous Judge, will give to me on that Day, and not to me only but also to all who have loved His appearing.*
>
> —2 TIMOTHY 4:6–8 (NKJV)

I have sometimes heard people as they get older come to a place of being ready to go to heaven or being willing to stay on earth to help others. For the believer, we know that while we are here in these earthly bodies, we are not at home with the Lord. But once we leave these earthly bodies, we will be at home with the Lord. (See 2 Corinthians 5:6–8.) Those who have had experiences where they went to heaven and returned said that they felt like they were "home." Such was the case of Dr. Mary Neal, an orthopedic surgeon from Wyoming.

Dr. Neal shares of an experience she had in January 1999. Dr. Neal and her husband, who is also a medical doctor, decided in celebrating their 26th wedding anniversary to do something different. Because they liked kayaking, they chose to take a week-long kayaking trip to the Los Rios region of Chile.

Her husband wasn't feeling well one day and said he would go to the lower part of the river where they would be landing their boats and read a book while he waited for the group. Dr. Neal said she was hesitant about going ahead, but others encouraged her so she went with the group.

The person in the kayak in front of her was not as experienced in kayaking and her boat turned sideways, so Dr. Neal went around her, but then unexpectedly went over a waterfall within a short distance. Her kayak went down into the water, lodging the front end of her kayak in rocks beneath. She could see the top of the water, but couldn't get out of her kayak because of the strong water current. She was running out of oxygen and realized she was going to drown.

Her friends came upon the scene and tried to free her, but couldn't get the boat unlodged from the rocks. She had a thought to relax instead of struggling.

Suddenly there was a shift with the boat, and her friends helped her get free. The current sucked her out of the bottom of the boat, bending her legs back over her knees. She could feel her bones breaking and her ligaments and tissues tearing.

As her friends helped to get her ashore, she realized she had left her body. She saw her friends do CPR on her body, trying to get her to breathe and she heard them calling her name. Her body was purple and bloated. Her eyes were fixed and dilated. She thought she must be dead.

She knew she had not been a very spiritual person. She attended church with her family, but didn't really seek the Lord. At that same moment, she was met by two people or two spirit beings who were so happy and began guiding her upward toward a lighted path. As she went up, she felt happy.

Then she had a thought about her husband, her children back home, and the patients she had at her medical clinic. But then she turned toward the light and again experienced such joy.

As she got closer to what looked like a dome structure with brilliant light all around it exploding with color and with love, she said she felt like she was "home." The spirit beings had not spoken before this, but then they stopped and said that she must go back because it was not her time to die. They said she still had work to do on earth.

Immediately she was back in her body breathing again. She had been without oxygen for thirty minutes, but had no brain damage. Her recovery of broken bones and ligaments took some months to heal.

After this experience, Dr. Neal said she knew she had to share with her family, friends, patients, and others the reality of heaven. She later wrote it in a book, *To Heaven and Back*.

If you have been struggling with your loved one dying and leaving you, I want to help you. When you have had a loving relationship together, you need to know they still love you dearly, but when people pass into eternity, *the draw of heaven* is so strong. They realize they have returned to where they came from.

In Jeremiah 1:5 God spoke to Jeremiah, "Before I formed [you] in the belly, I knew [you]...." When Christians die, they are escorted by heavenly spirit beings to heaven (Luke 16:22; Hebrews 1:13–14, 12:22–23). Our loved ones become surrounded by love that is beyond what we can understand here on earth. "God is love" (1 John 4:8). Love originates from Him. His love is perfect. There is no disappointment, nothing missing, nothing lacking in His love, but instead His love is everything we need or want.

Our loved one is grateful to be at home in God's presence. They believe that you will join them some day and be reunited with them. When you get there, you will understand as they do and you will have experienced *the draw of heaven* that they felt. I believe our loved ones still pray for us here on earth, because the spirit of Jesus lives inside of them. Romans 8:34 says that Jesus prays for us continually.

I believe they are praying for us to have a strong finish in this race that we have been called to run here on earth. They know that this world as we know it is going to come to an end one day, and there is a world to be reached before that day comes.

Once we accept Jesus' lordship in our lives, we are awakened to His calling on our lives. Second Timothy 1:9 says that He saved us and called us with a holy calling ("holy" meaning we have been consecrated, set apart for Him), not according to our works (not because of ourselves or whatever has happened in our lives apart from salvation), but according to His own purpose and grace which were given to us in Christ Jesus before the world began.

God has a purpose for us to be living on earth. We are not to just exist or survive day to day. He wants to use our lives, our strengths, our weaknesses, our gifts, and abilities, our personality, our life stories and all that He has given to us to bring His Kingdom into the lives of others.

We have only been given one life to live here on earth. Paul wrote in Ephesians 5:15 (AMPC), "Live purposefully." To live with purpose is to live your life full of meaning—thinking about what you do, how you are relating to others, recognizing that you have an influence upon others' lives.

I remember years ago hearing Brother Oral Roberts speak about Matthew 22:14: "Many are called, but few are chosen." He said that he believed that all of us are called according to other scriptures, but few choose the calling.

Life is made up of choices. We choose our responses to situations that happen in our lives. We have the ability to choose to allow God's Word to work His will in our lives. He then gives us His grace (His empowerment, help, strength, and favor) to do whatever we are called to do.

All through life, heaven has a draw upon our lives to do God's will and to do the works of Jesus as we reach out to touch the lives of others with His love. Just as Jesus said:

"I can of mine own self do nothing."

JOHN 5:30

"The Father that dwells in Me does the works."

JOHN 14:10, NKJV

"He that believeth on me, the works that I do shall he do also; and greater works than these shall he do; because I go unto my Father."

JOHN 14:12

Chapter 19

HEAVEN IS ON ITS FEET

(SEEING THE HARVEST)

I N JANUARY 1996, MY husband was preparing to speak at a men's breakfast meeting when the Spirit of God came upon him as he was standing and worshiping the Lord with others. (I shared this briefly in a previous chapter.) He said that he began to convulse with tears pouring from his eyes as he had a vision of being surrounded by a great cloud of witnesses. At this moment, he turned in his Bible to Hebrews 12:1–2 (NKJV) and read:

> Therefore we also, since we are surrounded by so great a cloud of witnesses, let us lay aside every weight, and the sin which so easily ensnares us, and let us run with endurance the race that is set before us, looking unto Jesus, the author and finisher of our faith, who for the joy that was set before Him endured the cross, despising the shame, and has sat down at the right hand of the throne of God.

Billy Joe said immediately that he was reminded of the fourth quarter of a football game when the two-minute warning is given.

When the score is close, the crowd stands spontaneously to its feet, and they do not sit down for the remainder of the game as they cheer on their team. He said that he sensed that "the cloud of witnesses" in heaven was on their feet with their faces pressed against what looked like a membrane material, cheering us on in our spiritual race.

Suddenly, the worship leader stopped leading worship and said, "Men, there is a great cloud of witnesses surrounding us. It's time to lay aside every sin and weight that has tripped us up."

At that moment, Billy Joe heard these words in his spirit: *Heaven is on its feet.* We are in the final part of the race of these last days. The cloud of witnesses started what we are to finish, and they are cheering for us to finish the race and finish strong to reach the goal that has been set before us.

Think about it! That was in 1996. The prophetic signs of the end times that the Bible has spoken about are around us. They indicate that the clock is ticking away and time is running out.

Many times people don't think that their loved ones in heaven are watching them on earth, but this scripture lets us know that they are interested in us here on earth. They know what time it is. They know that time is running out. They are on their feet. They aren't sitting around on clouds. They are preparing for what is ahead.

Many believe that our calculation of time is off somewhat. The time frame we are aware of for man's existence and governing on earth is around 6,000 years. Second Peter 3:8 says, "That with the Lord one day is as a thousand years, and a thousand years as one day." Many Bible scholars have compared man's time on earth to that of creation and that after God created the world in six days, He rested on the seventh day. The seventh day is said to be the seventh thousand years or the new millennium.

When our world entered the year AD 2000, people were very aware that we were passing an important mark in time. There has definitely been an escalation of biblical prophecy being fulfilled all around us. Those who have surrendered their lives to Jesus are expecting His return in the skies to raise up the saints on earth to meet Him. Scripture speaks of Jesus returning in the skies and believers being caught up together to meet Him in the air (1 Thessalonians 4:13–18).

The Bible tells us that a time will come when this world will go through a seven-year period of great tribulation (Revelation 18:1, 12:13–14, 13:5; Daniel 12:7).

After this, Jesus will return with the saints to set His feet on the earth and fight the final battle of the ages—the Battle of Armageddon (Revelation 19:11–21; Zechariah 14:2–9). Jesus will then set up His Kingdom on earth. There will be a new heaven and a new earth. The first heavens and earth will be done away with, and there will be a new city of Jerusalem from which Christ will rule over the nations (Revelation 21:1–3). Right now, we are experiencing the beginning of end-time events that Jesus prophesied would take place before the end would come.

When the disciples asked Jesus when His second coming and the end of the world would be, Jesus told them about signs that would be indicators (Matthew 24; Mark 13; Luke 21). Some of those signs will be:

1.   There will be those claiming to be the Messiah who are not.

2. False prophets will also arise to deceive some people.

3. Nations and kingdoms of the earth will rise against each other.

4. There will be earthquakes and famines in many places. All of these would be like the beginning of birth pains.

5. Jesus said those who were committed to Him would be hated, some tortured, and some killed around the world. There would be persecution.

6. Many will be offended.

7. Mark 13:9 says some will be dragged into courts and falsely accused.

8. Luke 21:16 TLB—Even some family members will betray one another.

9. Because sin will increase, the love of many will grow cold.

10. This gospel of the Kingdom will be preached in all the world, and then the end will come. Those who endure to the end will be saved.

The disciples had thought all of these things would happen when they were living on earth, but God desires a large family, and as time has passed, He has brought more people into the earth. He has also had men and women through the ages whom He has used to be His messengers to proclaim the gospel message and draw people to Him.

When the day of Pentecost happened after Jesus had risen from the dead and the disciples experienced the outpouring of the Holy Spirit (Acts 2:17), Peter stood and proclaimed that this was the fulfillment of what Joel had prophesied in Joel 2:28 about the last days. That was the first outpouring of the Holy Spirit, and His power came in His people to do the works of Jesus and reach people with the gospel message.

Since then, the Holy Spirit has moved within the lives of people around the world. Now we are in the final days of the outpouring of His Spirit on hungry hearts everywhere on the earth.

Using the analogy of farming, a farmer has to have a large rain to soak the ground when planting seed. Then he needs small rains over time as the crop begins to grow. But before the final harvest comes in, he has to have another great outpouring of rain to bring in a great harvest. This is where we are now.

We are to know the signs of the times we are in and the season of His Spirit moving in the earth so we will be willing to hear heaven's call and obey Him in this hour. The greatest sign Jesus spoke of is that this gospel of the Kingdom must be preached in all the world as a witness to all nations before the end.

Churches, Bible schools, Christian schools, rescue homes, orphanages, television, Internet, books, and using humanitarian aid to open the door to the gospel—all of these are helping to build the ark of safety for the lost to be saved in this final hour.

I remember in 2006 my late husband and I were in conversation one day with Brother Oral Roberts. We asked him his thoughts about the times we were in at that moment in relationship to the end-time

Scriptures. He said as bad as the world seemed at that time, we had not come to the place that Matthew 24:37–39 and Genesis 6:11 indicated was to happen.

Matthew 24:37–39 (CEV) says:

> *When the Son of Man appears, things will be just as they were when Noah lived. People were eating, drinking, and getting married right up to the day that the flood came and Noah went into the big boat. They didn't know anything was happening until the flood came and swept them all away. That is how it will be when the Son of Man appears.*

The *Amplified Translation* of these verses says:

> *As were the days of Noah, so will be the coming of the Son of Man.*
>
> *For just as in those days before the flood they were eating and drinking, [men] marrying and [women] being given in marriage, until the [very] day when Noah went into the ark.*
>
> *And they did not know or understand until the flood came and swept them all away—so will be the coming of the Son of Man.*

Genesis 6:11 (MSG) says:

> *As far as God was concerned, the Earth had become a sewer; there was violence everywhere. God took one look and saw how bad it was, everyone corrupt and corrupting—life itself corrupt to the core.*

This verse in the *Amplified Translation* reads:

The earth was depraved and putrid in God's sight, and the land was filled with violence (desecration, infringement, outrage, assault, and lust for power).

It appears we are now much closer to that time with corruption and violence filling the earth.

Before 2013, the majority of people in the world didn't know who ISIS was. The U. S. president at the time said they were just a small JV team of terrorists not to be concerned about. However, they grew through social media and began recruiting from around the world. Many of their recruits weren't religious, but just wanted to kill.

Radical Islam is fueled by Islamic leaders who tell their followers the Quran requires Islam to infiltrate and dominate all the nations of the world before their Mahdi (a type of Messiah) can return and rule the world. They are told they do this through violent and cultural jihad.

We have to realize that Islam is not just a religion. It is also a political system. Cultural jihad promotes the idea of establishing communities of Islam and then obtaining government positions so they can change government laws to Sharia law. Sharia law gives permission to Muslims to lie to non-Muslims. In fact, one of the names of Allah is "The Great Deceiver." Deception is a way of life for those who are committed to Sharia law and to preparing the way for their Mahdi.

The Western world has never understood the Islamic ideology. The Western world believes if you are nice and try to negotiate with people who hate you, they will respond affirmatively. However, radical Islam sees this as submission to Allah and an open door to domination.

Jesus spoke of deception and persecution in these last days (Matthew 24; Mark 13; Luke 21). Humanism is another deceptive factor in the world today, rejecting God's authority and man making his own laws. When leaders of nations have rejected Judeo-Christian beliefs to embrace humanism, it opened the way of vulnerability for others to come in and take over with terrorism. Christianity is the only belief that can change a person's heart from evil to good. Jesus is the only One who can replace love within a heart where hatred has been.

Paul wrote that in these last days, there would be a fierceness toward those who do good and an antichrist spirit that would seek to remove moral boundaries from society as a whole (2 Timothy 3:2–4).

In 2013 the U. S. Supreme Court legalized same-sex marriage. At first, states were told that each state would vote, indicating what their people wanted to do regarding the issue. Our state and others voted against it, but then a federal judge pushed it through beyond our citizens' votes to okay it. Then the Supreme Court voted to make it law. This meant it had to be taught in schools, but Christianity was not allowed to be taught or to mention the name of Jesus Christ.

Those who have pushed for legalizing same sex marriage are also pushing for acceptance and legalization of transgenderism. They push to allow them to use the bathrooms/showers of their choice of gender in schools, military, public places, etc.

In the midst of an antichrist spirit and an anti-morality and anti-government attitude, people still need Jesus. And God will use us, His Church, to be led by His Spirit and reach people for Him.

HIV, Aids, and Hepatitis, along with other sexually transmitted diseases, are rampant among those who choose an immoral lifestyle.

But the media doesn't want to mention it. Many who have been addicted to drugs, along with their immoral lifestyle, are seeing their bodies deteriorating. Some are dying early deaths. Abuse, sex trafficking, porn, immoral nightclubs, prostitution, etc. all feed into the corruption of the world system. God wants to save people, set them free, and heal them inside and out.

We are called to fulfill God's vision for reaching the harvest in these last days. That harvest is people who need His saving grace. God doesn't change the vision because of changing times or intensity of the enemy's hindrances or his attacks, or a wavering economy.

Jesus told the disciples not to say, "There are still four months and then the harvest." He said in John 4:35 (NKJV), "Lift up your eyes and look at the fields, for they are already white for harvest." This was the last thing my husband wrote and left on his desk at our house. John 4:37 ERV continues: "It is true when we say. 'One person plants, but another person harvests the crop.'"

Jesus has called every believer to work the fields, to be His witness here in the earth, and to help bring people to Him to be saved before they step into eternity.

When Jesus looked at people, He was moved with compassion to save them, heal them, set them free, and work supernatural miracles in their lives. He came to show people the truth, to show what real life is, and to show the way to the Father.

Jesus still is moved with compassion for people. He sees the world groping in darkness. That's why He has called us to be the light of the world and a city set on a hill. We are to stand out so obviously that people are attracted to the light we have. We are to know the message so we can share it and share how it has changed our lives. Since Jesus now lives in us, the Holy Spirit has put that same love and compassion inside of us to reach people.

The enemy wants to stop God's plan in reaching the harvest, so he creates hindrances in Christians' lives, such as:

1. Distractions.

2. Busyness—Keeping us busy with cares of life, causing us to forget the harvest.

3. Thoughts of fear—Causing us to not reach out beyond ourselves to others because we might be rejected.

4. Thoughts that someone else will do it and it won't be a necessity for you, because God loves you anyway.

5. Thoughts that evangelism is not your gifting. You have other giftings.

6. Thoughts that you haven't been trained to witness.

7. Thoughts that your past is so bad you should let others do the witnessing. Jesus will use every available vessel (person) to share His message of love and hope. He knows that your testimony will impact someone else to receive Him.

Acts 2:17 states that in the last days God will pour out His Spirit upon all flesh and sons and daughters, the young and old, men and women, would prophesy. The day of Pentecost was the beginning of the last days. We are now in the latter part of the last days, and heaven is pouring out the Holy Spirit on hungry hearts around the world.

God is drawing people to Himself through believers who are unashamed of the testimony of Jesus Christ. In John 12:32 Jesus said, "And I, if I be lifted up from the earth, will draw all men unto me." You and I are still here on earth with purpose. That purpose is to awaken the hearts of people that we come in contact with to see that their needs can only be met in Jesus.

Recently, I heard a testimony of a lady who is now an active member of our church. She was hooked on drugs for 19 years and lost her family and everything that she had during that time. She came to a place of seeing her life could only be changed through faith in Jesus Christ. She received Jesus and was delivered from drug addiction. Now, she has seen Jesus restore her life over the past few years, and she's involved in everything we have offered for discipleship. God has used her to witness to others.

Jesus takes whatever mess we have had in our past and turns it into a message to give others hope in Him. He takes the story of our tests and turns it into a testimony to encourage others to realize they can overcome. Our testimony then becomes a prophetic word that He uses to impact others around us. Revelation 19:10 says, "The testimony of Jesus is the spirit of prophecy."

Matthew 5:13 (MSG) says, "Let me tell you why you are here. You're here to be salt—seasoning that brings out the God-flavors of this earth. If you lose your saltiness, how will people taste godliness? . . ."

Salt has many functions. It gives flavor and it seasons. It can improve the taste of food. You season the atmosphere wherever you are. You improve difficult situations where other people are involved because you believe in God's supernatural power.

Just as salt melts ice, your love can melt the hardest of hearts. Salt heals. You have the healing power of Jesus Christ in you to pray for those who are sick and release your faith for a miracle. Salt preserves, and as long as Christians are in this world, we are preserving it and restraining the spirit of iniquity from taking over the world. Salt is found everywhere, and God has His people everywhere around the world.

As I mentioned earlier, the last thing that my husband wrote on a legal pad was the scripture from John 4:35. It was lying on his desk. Jesus said, "Do you not say, 'There are still four months and then comes the harvest'? Behold, I say to you, lift up your eyes and look at the fields, for they are already white for harvest!" (NKJV).

Billy Joe was aware of the harvest throughout his life. So many times he and I would either be at a gas station, a restaurant, or somewhere else out in public and he would start to talk to someone about the Lord. He inspired me and many others to not wait for someone to ask, but to be forward and friendly in starting a conversation with people and taking the conversation toward the Lord and asking if he could pray for them.

A Woman at a Well

Jesus was forward and friendly and would start a conversation with people wherever He was. When you read the whole chapter of John 4, you see how Jesus lived with an awareness. The disciples had gone into a nearby Samaritan town to buy food. Even though Jesus was tired, as

He rested by the well, He noticed a Samaritan woman who came to draw water from the well.

When you know your purpose in being here on earth, you know people need what you have.

After Jesus' conversation with the woman, she realized He could be the Messiah people were expecting to come. In fact, Jesus identified Himself to her as the Messiah. She ran to go and tell others in the town to come see Him, leaving her water pot.

The disciples returned with food and saw that He had been talking to this Samaritan woman, which was against Jewish law. They didn't know what to say so they urged Jesus to eat. Jesus replied that He had food that they didn't know about. They thought He was speaking of natural food. Then He said a very important word: "My food is to do the will of Him who sent Me, and to finish His work" (John 4:34, NKJV).

Jesus told His disciples not to wait around and say there was plenty of time before the harvest. He said, "Lift up your eyes and look at the fields, for they are already white for harvest" (v. 35, NKJV). Many times we get preoccupied with our own cares of life, and we do not see the people God puts in our pathway.

Are You Available for God to Use?

Years ago the Lord spoke to me through an experience I had regarding this scripture of seeing the harvest. My husband had asked me to go to the store to get one thing that he needed before leaving to go to the airport. He knew that I could get into conversations easy with people so he told me to just go in and get what he needed and come right back so we would get to the airport on time.

I went into the store and got the item. However, I passed a lady pushing a cart, and as I greeted her, she barely looked at me. She was very depressed. I was about to check out, and the Holy Spirit said, "Go back and pray for her."

I didn't know her, but I obeyed the voice of the Holy Spirit and had to search briefly to find her. I went to her and said that when I passed her, I felt I was to come back and ask if I could pray for her. She reluctantly said, "Well, okay."

After I prayed, I opened my eyes and tears were flowing down her face. She said, "You hit it right on the nail in your prayer." I hugged her and told her maybe one day I would find out what that nail was. Then I left. It only took about two or three minutes. I arrived home in time to take Billy Joe to the airport. I heard the Holy Spirit say to me, "I can work quickly if you will obey Me."

Many times we just need to lift up our eyes and look at people. We have to become aware of people. They have needs many times that they are hiding. Jesus wants to flow through us with insight that is beyond our own minds. He just needs our availability.

Don't Let Rejection Paralyze You

I remember not long after I had surrendered my life to Jesus at age 16, I was trying to share the gospel with a group of people. One of the people challenged me in front of everyone, and I didn't know what to say in response. I knew she didn't like me. I felt defeated. I didn't want to be around this group again, but I had a class at school with them so I had to be around them. I prayed for God to redeem my failure.

A few years later, after I was out of college, I ran into that person who had challenged me years before. I spoke to her, and she in turn was nice to me. I was somewhat surprised but thanked God for giving me another chance with her. We visited, and I invited her to a meeting we were having at a church nearby.

Don't Let Fear Hold You Back

Some people have a fear of not knowing what to say, feeling like they don't know enough of God's Word, but we have to start somewhere. I only knew John 3:16 and Psalm 100 from memory when I first witnessed to a girl. However, I knew I had had a personal experience with Jesus coming into my life and taking over, so I shared that with her; then I prayed with her and she received Jesus. Gradually I learned more scriptures to share with people.

Some people are just afraid to talk to others. Some listen to the negative news so much they think everyone is suspicious, so they stay away from people.

Others compare themselves to people thinking, "Who would want to listen to me?" Get past the comparison trap. I did the same thing during those first few years after I was saved. God spoke to my heart one day, and my Bible fell open to 2 Corinthians 10:12 (AMP), which says, "When they measure themselves with themselves and compare themselves with one another, they are without understanding and behave unwisely."

I was surprised when I saw this scripture, and I made a decision to purposefully not compare myself. At various times through the years, I had to remind myself of this scripture. That takes the pressure off of us when we decide to live by the Word.

I remember one time being invited by a friend into a secular setting in New York City where there were many famous people. I didn't know all the names of the people, but others knew them. At first, I felt out of place. I became aware of my simple dress that was not like the expensive gowns others wore.

Then I heard the Holy Spirit say to me, "You're here because they need what you've got." Immediately, I quit thinking about myself and began to make conversation with others around me, sharing miracle stories to create spiritual hunger in them. That's what Jesus did with the woman at the well.

In John 4, after Jesus had ministered to the Samaritan woman, He told His disciples that His meat was to do the will of the Father. Years ago, I heard certain people say, "I want to go to church where the pastor teaches the deep meat of God's Word." They went on to say that they wanted to know all the details of the background and the original meanings of the Scriptures.

There is nothing wrong with wanting to study Scripture, but Hebrews 5:11–14 indicates that those who just hear the Word taught, but do not use it to disciple others, become dull of hearing and spiritually lazy. They can't take the meat of God's Word, but instead have to be fed like a baby the milk of God's Word because they give into hindrances and offenses.

Those who disciple others learn to let go of offense and not let hindrances stop them. Their spiritual discernment and understanding are sharpened while ministering to people. Jesus said the meat of God's Word is doing the will of the Father.

Jesus went on to say that one person plants the seed of God's Word in a person's life, and another reaps the harvest. Sometimes we are planting seeds into people we talk with. Other times we get to reap the harvest by praying the salvation prayer with them. The main thing is to know from the Holy Spirit in each situation you are in if you are planting or reaping.

Heaven draws people through us. This is why Jesus told us to "raise our eyes and observe the fields." The fields represent people. He wants us to see people around us. When Jesus saw people, Scripture says He was moved with compassion to do something. Pity just feels sorry for people, but compassion does something to help people. Jesus saw the masses and had compassion toward them.

Both Matthew 9:36 and Mark 6:34 tell us that Jesus was moved with compassion when He saw the multitude of people because they were like sheep without a shepherd—no one to guide them in the right direction. He took time to teach them many things.

In Mark 6:35–44 Jesus was moved with compassion to feed the multitude that He taught. He performed the miracle of multiplying the five loaves and two fish, feeding more than 5,000 people, with fragments of food left over.

In Matthew 14:14 Jesus was moved with compassion when He saw the multitude bringing their sick to Him, and He healed them.

He saw individuals and had compassion toward them.

In Mark 1:41 Jesus was moved with compassion to touch and heal the leper. Others didn't want to touch him. Jesus wasn't afraid to touch the leper.

In Luke 7:12 Jesus had compassion when He saw a widow who only had one son and he had died. Jesus raised him from the dead.

In John 8:3–11 Jesus had compassion on the woman caught in adultery to forgive her, even though the law said she should be stoned.

In Luke 19:1–10 Jesus had compassion toward Zacchaeus who had been crooked, taking money wrongfully from people. Jesus went to his house to eat with him, and Zacchaeus was so convicted in his heart that he said he would repay all those he had taken from wrongfully and give them more than he had taken.

All of those that Jesus came in contact with experienced His love and His power. Heaven draws us to move in this same divine flow, reaching out to others.

Situations Where People Are Most Open to the Gospel

There are three situations that people go through when they are most open to the gospel:

1. When they need a miracle.

2. When they are in transition, such as when they have moved from one place to another or from one job situation to another; or they have changed schools and they don't know anyone yet in the school they have gone to; or possibly they have gone through a

divorce and they are now having to learn to live apart
from the other person.

3.   When they have gone through a loss—possibly a
      loved one has passed away, or they have lost their job
      or their house or their car; maybe they have lost a
      relationship.

In any of these settings, people are open to someone who shows
that he or she cares about them and their situation.

Paul told the Philippians that he was sending Timothy to minister
to them. He said he had no other person who was like-minded who
would naturally care for them. He said many others were seeking just
to take care of themselves and were not interested in taking responsibility for others (Philippians 2:20–21). God is looking for like-minded
Christians in this hour through whom He can draw people to Him.

He draws us to multiply what we have been given (Matthew
25:14–30: The parable of the talents). He draws us to watch and pray,
to walk in His authority, and to do the work He calls us to do (Mark
13:33–37).

Heaven draws us to be ready for Jesus' return (Matthew 25:1–13;
Mark 13:32–37).

Heaven draws us to help those in need, particularly His brethren,
the Jewish people (Matthew 25:31–46).

Heaven draws us to be as Jesus is in this world and not to fear. His
perfect love casts out all fear (1 John 4:17–18; John 14:12).

Heaven draws us to love one another the way He loves us (John
13:34–35; Romans 13:8).

Heaven draws us to never put a stumbling block or an occasion to fall in our brother's way (Romans 14:13).

Heaven draws us to come after Him, deny ourselves, take up our cross daily to follow Him and not be ashamed to confess Him before men so He will not be ashamed to confess us before our Father in heaven (Luke 9:23–26).

Heaven needs you and me. There is a divine flow with God. It is in following His love and leading. He will back us with His power if we will follow His lead and believe in His power.

After my husband died, I had been preaching in our services and praying for people to be saved, healed, and delivered. I knew people needed the power of God and miracles. Since my husband had died, I think people wondered if I would preach about healing and pray for the sick to be healed. I knew the Lord wanted me to.

On one occasion, a man was brought to our Wednesday night church service who had just gotten out of the hospital and was in a wheelchair. Because of drugs, he had been in a horrible motorcycle accident where a tractor trailer had run over him on his motorcycle. His mother had been praying for all of her family to be saved and delivered. He was no longer on the drugs and had prayed the salvation prayer.

That Wednesday night his mother wheeled him up to the front because he wanted me to pray for his healing and to come out of his wheelchair. I prayed and he carefully got up. When he sat back down in his chair, he told me that he was going to come out of that wheelchair and walk.

That weekend I was ministering in our Christmas production, and when I gave the invitation at the end of the presentation, I heard a voice from the back of the audience yell, "Pastor Sharon, watch this!" The man wheeled his wheelchair down front, locked it in place, and got up from it, and walked toward me on his own, praising God! I told the congregation his story, and everyone praised God!

Billy Joe's Guidelines for Reaching the Lost

My late husband said, "In order for God's people to reach this world, it will require:

1. A removal of selfishness in order to think about others and do something to make a difference in this world and advance God's Kingdom here on earth. For God's Kingdom to advance, God's people have to be willing to give financially to support missions." I believe God gifts men and women with business understanding to make money to advance His Kingdom. Sometimes people forget this and begin to hold onto the money for themselves. There is so much happening right now with missions. I know areas of missions where millions could be used immediately if people were willing to give.

2. A willingness to give our lives for the call and the cause of Jesus Christ.

3. We pray "Thy Kingdom come, thy will be done in earth as it is in heaven." We need to then expect

Heaven to work with us here on earth. God can lead us to the person that someone else has been praying for and now they're open to listen.

I've thought about two more requirements:

1. It will require faith to believe God and to reject the spirit of fear. The enemy wants to paralyze God's people with fear so they won't go where God desires. Faith believes in God's supernatural help.

2. It will require taking time to hear God's direction. Romans 8:14 says that those who are led by the Spirit of God are the sons and daughters of God. Hebrews 3:7–8 says that today if you hear God's voice, don't harden your heart. Don't resist His voice. Desire to hear from Him and follow His lead.

The Baton Is in Our Hands

In a mile relay race, there are four laps around the track and four runners. The first runner is a strong runner to get a good position. The second and third runners must run strategically, but the key to winning the relay is the last runner. He must be the fastest and the strongest.

Generations have come and gone before us. They have carried the torch—the flame of God's Spirit. They have stood in the face of opposition and remained strong. They have fought and won battles. They have moved in faith and obedience to God's voice. The baton is in our hands, and we are in the last leg of the race.

1.   You have a race to run, so run with *endurance*.

2.   You are called to reach out to people with *God's love*.
     John 13:35 says, "By this shall all men know that ye
     are my disciples, if ye have love one to another."

3.   There is a call to step out in *faith* and *do* what you
     have never done before, obeying God.

4.   *God will make up for your inadequacies* if you will be
     willing and obedient.

5.   Jesus said to four common men: "Follow Me, and I
     will make you become fishers of men" (Mark 1:17,
     NKJV). *Jesus makes us become whatever He calls us to do.*

Heaven is drawing every person in this hour to hear God's voice
and to follow His lead; to use what He has given to each of us to
advance His Kingdom here in the earth.

Hebrews 12:1 tells us to lay aside every weight and sin that would
try to trip us up. Run with an attitude of endurance (not quitting),
and keeping our focus on Jesus.

Philippians 3:14 (AMP) says, "Press on toward the goal to win the
[supreme and heavenly] prize to which God in Christ Jesus is calling
us upward."

Then one day we will be drawn over into eternity to be with the
Lord and to be reunited with loved ones who have stepped into eternity before us, and who have prayed for us and cheered for us to finish
strong.

My Husband's Greatest Motivation for Ministry and for All of Life: The Harvest

In the race for eternity, especially in his last years on earth, my late husband, Billy Joe Daugherty, made every step of his life count for eternity. He was motivated by the harvest of people. He spent his life sharing Jesus with as many people as he possibly could.

To the person sitting next to him on an airplane or to tens of thousands of people at a crusade, at the gas station, a funeral or wedding, or when a camera was rolling, he believed every occasion was the right one for sharing Jesus and that is what he did.

Today, Pastor Billy Joe is among the great cloud of witnesses. Heaven is on its feet, cheering us on in our race to win the lost.

Chapter 20

FINISHING STRONG

I have fought the good fight, I have finished the race, and I have remained faithful.

—2 Timothy 4:7 (NLT)

MORE THAN ANYTHING, GOD wants us to finish strong while we are here on earth. This means we must live purposefully. Ephesians 5:17 (NLT) says that we are not to live thoughtlessly, but we are to understand what is God's will for our lives and then walk it out. "Living with heavenly vision is essential to running your race well" (John Bevere).

Have you ever heard someone say, "He or she is so heavenly minded that they are no earthly good"? If you stop to think about that statement, it isn't a true evaluation of someone. What they are trying to say is that that person may go to church and have a show of religion, but he or she doesn't relate to people who need help and need the Lord.

In reality, if we set our minds on heaven or eternity, it will affect how we relate to people here on earth in a positive way, because we will have heaven's heart toward people.

Colossians 3:2 tells us to set our affections on the things above and not on the things here below, where Christ is seated at the right hand of God. Then it goes on to say that we are not to allow lust to dominate our lives. We are to refuse giving in to anger, rage, sexual lawlessness, greed, slander, dirty language, being malicious, lying or being deceitful.

The reason for this is that when a person has no boundaries in these areas, they will end up hurting themselves and hurting others.

Remove the Weights

> *Therefore, since we are surrounded by such a huge crowd of witnesses to the life of faith, let us strip off every weight that slows us down, especially the sin that so easily trips us up. And let us run with endurance the race God has set before us.*
>
> *We do this by keeping our eyes on Jesus, the champion who initiates and perfects our faith. Because of the joy awaiting him, he endured the cross, disregarding its shame. Now he is seated in the place of honor beside God's throne.*
>
> —HEBREWS 12:1–2 (NLT)

I remember a guy in high school who lived out in the country. He played sports and he worked out at home by running out in his fields with weights on his ankles. Then he would take off the weights so he could run fast.

Our lives are lighter when we get rid of weights of sin, weights of offense and unforgiveness, or weights of cares of this life. Be determined to stay in the race and continue in God's will at times when it is difficult. That's endurance. This is an endurance race—not a sprint.

In Acts 20:24 (NKJV), Paul had heard from the Holy Spirit that he was to go to Jerusalem, and he knew that there were people who wanted to kill him because of his preaching the gospel message. Others tried to urge him not to go, but to stay where things were safe and convenient. The race He calls us to isn't always easy.

Sometimes God has us do things that seem risky to other people, but God always has a reason for reaching people anytime He speaks to us to do something out of the ordinary.

Paul knew he might be imprisoned, but he said, "None of these things move me, nor do I count my life dear to myself, so that I might finish my race with joy…" (Acts 20:24, NKJV).

There is a reward at the end of our lives when we obey the Lord. The key to finishing our race is keeping our focus on Jesus. There will be times when people will not meet your expectations. This is why we keep our eyes on Jesus and His Word. Meditating God's Word not only changes our way of thinking, but it keeps our thoughts right.

Our thoughts control our bodies. It has been said, "Where the mind goes, the body follows." Proverbs 23:7 (NKJV) says, "For as he thinks in his heart, so is he…."

We can take control of our lives by taking control of our thoughts. We take control of our thoughts by meditating, memorizing, and speaking what God's Word says. Once we begin to do this, when a wrong thought comes to our mind, we speak to it and cast it down with our words.

> *For though we walk in the flesh, we do not war after the flesh:*
> *(For the weapons of our warfare are not carnal, but mighty*
> *through God to the pulling down of strong holds;)*

Casting down imaginations, and every high thing that exalteth itself against the knowledge of God, and bringing into captivity every thought to the obedience of Christ;

And having in a readiness to revenge all disobedience, when your obedience is fulfilled.

—2 Corinthians 10:3-6

We can reject wrong thoughts and speak to them to go in Jesus' name. And we can speak what God's Word says to renew our thinking in the right direction.

Living the Life of Love

When we realize our lives not only are about us but about how we affect others, it changes our way of life and our view of things. Jesus told His disciples He was giving a new commandment. It was the commandment of love. This kind of love was not a romantic type of love, but the God-kind of love which is selfless, giving and sacrificial. It is the kind of love that does what will benefit others before itself. It is unconditional love that goes beyond offense and hurt. It is a love that considers others' needs and considers how others are affected by choices that are made.

Romans 13:8–10 tells us that when we truly love God and love others, we won't steal, kill, lie against others, covet what they have, or commit sexual sin because all of this hurts others. He says love works no ill against someone else, and we are called to live by the law of God's love.

The heart of heaven is love as stated in John 3:16: "For God so loved the world, that he gave his only Son, that whosoever believeth in him, should not perish, but have everlasting life."

God loves the people of this world. His Son Jesus paid the price on the cross to free us from sin's power, and He gave us a newness of life through His resurrection from the dead. He is not just a religion. He is a relationship with supernatural power to cleanse sin, deliver people from addictions or bondage, heal people, and restore lives to fulfill His purpose here on earth.

We have this message of hope and freedom to change lives and impact our world, and God needs every one of us.

Finishing strong is not only about living our lives in a right direction, but it is also about recognizing we are here on earth with purpose. We aren't here just to take up space. We aren't just a spare part. We aren't here just to survive. God has a reason for you and me being here. He has gifted each of us in different ways to use those gifts to influence and help others in this world around us.

God needs you and me. We are all a part of a greater plan than we can even see. It takes effort to get out of your comfort zone and find a place to serve others, but when you do, you will feel so rewarded later on. One day we will stand before God and give an account for our obedience to His voice here on earth. We want to hear Him say, "Well done, good and faithful servant. Enter into the joy of the Lord" (Matthew 25:21).

Whereas you do not know what will happen tomorrow. For what is your life? It is even a vapor that appears for a little time and then vanishes away.

—JAMES 4:14 (NKJV)

Life goes by quickly. I've heard it said that life is a gift. We can waste it on drugs, alcohol, partying, gambling, and living aimlessly. We can spend it on accumulating a lot of material possessions, becoming highly successful in the corporate world, acquiring degrees for notoriety, and making more and more money. Or we can invest it by making a difference here on earth in impacting the lives of others.

The late Dr. Myles Munroe wrote, "Your life isn't measured by *duration* but by *donation*. Live your life with purpose—to change this world." I agree with this statement. Stop and think about your life. What are you doing that is having a positive effect on others on a regular basis? How are you helping to bring change to the world around you in a better way?

When you go to a cemetery, you will see grave markers. They have the name of a person and underneath the name it says DOB (date of birth)—DOD (date of death). How will you live between your DOB and your DOD? Some people never think about how they will live their life. They just live for the moment. Moments, however, add up to days that add up to months that become years. Your life can take a sudden change in a moment, but if you make a decision right now at this moment to live your life for God's purposes, you won't have any regrets in the end.

I know this was settled in me when my husband passed away. I knew, "For to me to live is Christ..." (Philippians 1:21). I had a supernatural peace that somehow God was going to work in our lives and through our lives as a family, as a staff, and as a church.

When I look at our family who are all in ministry, our staff, our schools, and congregation, and all who have gone out from Victory into other parts of the world, we've embraced God's calling. We've chosen to lift up our eyes and see the harvest to reach them.

When a loved one dies, we who are still here on earth are faced with the question, "What are we going to do now?" Life goes on. I suggest that you find a place where you can give love to others who need you and your gifts or abilities.

When we give out of our own need, we end up receiving back into our lives. I have experienced this time and time again in a variety of ways.

You don't have to be a celebrity or have titles to do extraordinary things for God and His Kingdom. Just say, "Lord, have Your way in my life. Show me what You want me to do and I'll do it."

If you say, "God can't use me," that is an insult to God. He doesn't use you for who you are or what you have accomplished. He uses you to show His power.

It's time to say, "Lord, here am I. Use me. Help me, Lord, to finish my course with joy" (Acts 20:24).

God planted eternity in our hearts the moment we were placed on earth (Ecclesiastes 3:11). Some attempt to drown out that calling from heaven. But if we will listen, heaven calls us to fulfill God's purpose while living here on earth—to finish our race. People's lives are on the other end of our obedience to God. Stay in the race. Get up if you were knocked down. The baton has been passed to us by those who are now in Heaven watching us, wanting us to finish strong. There is a draw of heaven upon our lives and there's grace to fulfill His will.

ARE YOU READY FOR HEAVEN?

Possibly you need to surrender your life to Jesus right now. Maybe you prayed a salvation prayer before. This prayer is a prayer of surrender and a prayer to receive God's grace to help you go forward.

Lord Jesus, thank You for dying on the cross for me and for rising from the dead for me. I believe in You, and I receive Your lordship in my life. I surrender to You.

I let go of disappointment, hurt, and pain. I receive Your healing deep within my soul. I receive Your purpose and direction in my heart. I believe You are with me. You will never leave me or abandon me.

I ask You to fill me with Your Holy Spirit. Baptize me in Your power. I choose to let go of fear, worry, and insecurity. I believe You have a good plan for my life. I let go of every weight that would try to hinder me from running the race You have set before me.

Use my life to touch others with Your love and to help others know the power of Your grace. Help me to finish my race with joy, and give me grace to overcome in the days ahead, in Your name I pray, Jesus. Amen!

ABOUT THE AUTHOR

Sharon Daugherty and her late husband, Billy Joe Daugherty, are the founding pastors of Victory Christian Center in Tulsa, Oklahoma. Victory serves as the hub of an international television, radio, Internet ministry, along with planting Bible Institutes and churches globally. Their mission program supports and sends out missionaries and humanitarian aid throughout the world through their mission program and Victory Bible College. Sharon is a speaker, teacher, worship leader and author, including several books, such as *Known by Your Fruit, Avoiding Deception* and others.

Sharon is the Oklahoma State Director of Christians United for Israel and a graduate of Oral Roberts University. She spends most of her time traveling and speaking throughout the world, teaching and encouraging the body of Christ in reaching the lost, preparing for the times we live in, and bringing the generations together for the sake of the Gospel.